IN THE NAME OF *LOVE*

In the Name of Love
©2014 by Kathleen Rioux

All rights reserved. No part of this publication may be reproduced, distributed, or transmitted in any form or by any means, including photocopying, recording, or other electronic or mechanical methods, without the prior written permission of the publisher, except in the case of brief quotations embodied in critical reviews and certain other noncommercial uses permitted by copyright law.

This is a work of nonfiction. The people and characters in this book are real and have been portrayed as accurately as possible. The author apologizes in advance for errors or inconsistencies.

Parts of this book previously appeared in 2014 as *Thunder Moon*

Published by Piscataqua Press
An imprint of RiverRun Bookstore 142 Fleet St.
Portsmouth, NH 03801

ISBN: 9781950381470

Cover image: depositphotos/heckmannoleg

Printed in the U.S.A.

In the Name of Love

A memoir by

Kathleen Rioux

The GLORY is not
In never FAILING, BUT
In the RISING every time You FALL…

—Chinese Proverb

This memoir is dedicated to my daughters who are the loves of my life. The miracles that help my soul to soar, to sing! They are angelic heroes who have allowed me to hear my own music. So very, very, very grateful to be able to share time with them.

I Love you all-ways, always

Mom

FOREWORD

ON JUNE 13th, 2001, fear devoured me. I had reached out for help, to the community and others, but help did not come. Suffering from PTSD, which I was later diagnosed with, my adrenaline-saturated blood drove me to do something totally out of character. I was so sick I went beyond reason, and purchased a handgun to take my life.

Just like all the weather conditions necessary in creating a horrific tsunami, a troubled past had left me deeply vulnerable—a belief system of worthlessness. This made it easy for me to slip down a destructive path, making poor decisions that included choosing toxic male relationships.

Unfortunately, suicidal became homicidal. I felt I needed to right what was wrong, like an evangelist, and stop the predator from hurting anyone else. On June 14, 2001, five shots were fired, with one left for me.

We all have a story to tell, and this memoir is my story. It is not about being a victim, or looking for revenge. It is a story about survival and courage, and in the words of Winston Churchill, "Never, never, never giving up."

I hope that I will be understood, not judged. No one was in my shoes. Oprah once said, "Forgiveness is giving up the hope that the past could have been different." And, the first person I had to forgive was myself. I am still a work in progress.

PART ONE:

THUNDER MOON

ONE

ON ONE PARTICULAR day, in one particular month, in one particular year, a silent moon rumbled the truth for the hearts of those in charge to hear, and in the name of love, a sentencing was set forth for a young woman. It was not the power of the golden harvest moon, or the brilliant blue moon, or even the banana shaped quarter moon. On no, it was the mighty Thunder Moon!

I AM ALIVE! I AM ALIVE! I say to myself, for comfort, I guess. To affirm the decision I had made one night, in June of 2001. I was supposed to be going to listen to a group known as the Cider Press Band, in New Boston, in a frenzy of freedom, freedom from an abusive situation; meanwhile, fate was making other plans.

Lynne Beernhert, the friend who had taken me in and supplied me with shelter from the storm in my life, along with a few of her friends, had all made plans to see the band as we headed out to celebrate my newfound independence.

We headed to one of the local watering holes in downtown Manchester, NH, the Black Brimmer. Unfortunately, Lynne and her friends did not know the torture I had gone through, or how much I had taken, the things that I had gotten, and hadn't even ask for.

Yes, I was physically free of a horrific situation—but mentally, I was still trapped there; independence scared the HELL out of me, believe it or not! The only way I can describe it now is like a soldier coming home from war. While you are in it, you operate in survival mode. Shell shocked, the trauma that you experience can come back in full force, just like you are back in it, even though you are safe and sound somewhere.

Fear in its rawest form!

Fight or flight, pure and simple.

So, there was a change of plans on this evening. For here I sit in the Valley Street Jail.

JAIL, as I write the word I feel as though I've cursed.

I'M LOCKED IN a 7' by 13' cell. I know for sure the precise size, because I've walked around this cage enough times. I have been confined to this cell for five days. FIVE DAYS! With only two hours out a day to shower and make a phone call to anyone who could or would except a collect call from me. All calls you make are collect because you don't have any money, or credit cards.

As my blood began to cool, the reality hit me square between the eyes, as I slowly became aware of where I was and what I had done! It was all a horrific nightmare come true. It was beyond comprehension. The seriousness of my actions, and the consequences, were drowning my thoughts. There were no activities, no counseling or anything to distract me. Left with only my thoughts, I began to struggle with the probable outcome of all of this. At that time, I believed that I would rather be dead than to be sent to prison, which was a strong possibility. My black and white thinking took over any hope I had, and I wanted to die.

I attempted suicide the second day of my confinement. I had no weapons, so I could think of only two methods for my demise. The first thing that came to mind was the bottom partial from my mouth. It was sharp, with jagged edges. I could puncture the main artery in my neck. Bleed to death.

I tried it. I couldn't do it that way. I was too chicken!

The next attempt was not to drink any water. I would be dead within ten days. Yes, ten days is the longest a human being can go without water. I knew I had heard or read that somewhere. It was a sure thing. However, by day three I was developing sores inside my mouth, and I could hardly swallow. I had to talk to my lawyer and had to be able to speak. You can't speak very well when your mouth is dry and parched. Surely, I did not want Mr. Swope to suspect me of being, well, SUICIDAL. The irony is that someone who really wants to kill themselves, can; they never tell anyone they are going to do it either. If they do tell, they usually want to live, not die!

I know now how very sick I was, but I was in shock! Physically and mentally in desperate need of hospitalization. Instead, due to the laws, I was punished with incarceration! My lawyer knew what the predator had done to me, and yet not a single blood test was done or a cervical exam.

Nothing! Such treatment is a terrible, terrible, terrible thing to do to any human being!

PALE YELLOW WALLS surround me, holding me here. The world outside, versus the world here within. One is worse than the other. Which one right now?

The tan concrete floor greets my feet every time I stand to walk, to jog (helps for the sanity), to do yoga, or to go to the bathroom—out in the open mind you—and to wash my face and hands or brush my teeth.

The stainless-steel toilet is in the corner, an open bowl, with no lid. A matching minuscule sink, the size of a cereal bowl, also occupies some of the 7' by 13' floor space.

A grayish blue steel bunk bed, attached to the wall, holds my frail 97-pound body up at night to sleep, hardly, to read mostly, to write, to do sit-ups, and of course to PRAY! The bunk bed is secured to the concrete walls by huge bolts.

The door to the cell is solid steel, about eight inches thick. There are no handles on the door, and it has a very small window top center. The Correctional Officers are in charge of the opening and closing of it. I'm thinking that even the Incredible Hulk couldn't have gotten himself out of here.

Every time the door is opened or closed it makes a thunderous clunk, a haunting reminder of where I am, especially when newly arrested women enter into the secured facility in the wee hours of the morning.

On the sixth day I joined the regular jail population. I guess I was a little too IRREGULAR on the first five days. I needed to be tamed.

It was a major shock, my first visit. It would be my last too!

The sections we are on are referred to as pods.

There is only one pod for women. Right now, there are about 30 women here, some in desperate need of psychiatric attention. They really don't belong here, in my opinion, but evidently there is no place for them in the state.

We can't have dental floss because we might try to commit suicide. We are, however, supplied with razor blades to shave our legs. Go figure!

When street people are brought in, they do not check them for contagious diseases. For example, head lice. One woman came in unchecked and spread lice to others on our pod! One of the inmates was fixing the others hair and noticed them. So disgusting! So, we all began to check one another. There were about three cases discovered at that time.

The nurse that came on duty that day, which was a Saturday I believe, was told about the situation. She told us that she would take care of it. Days passed and nothing was done. I mean, all the women wanted was the shampoo to rid themselves of these pests! Simple enough you would think! Evidently, the nurse had done absolutely nothing.

Several days later two other women came down with head lice.

Because there is no healing that takes place here at the Valley Street Jail, like activities or any counseling, the women develop a fragility that allows for the least bit of stress to put them over the edge. Rightly so! The phrase, "The straw that broke the camel's back," is one that rings true for most of the women here.

So, this very young woman, her name escapes me, brought the lice problem to the attention of a professional, who never followed through (I guess us criminal types don't deserve any respect!). The very woman who reported the lice problem ended up getting them. Unfortunately for her, this was the STRAW that broke her back. She freaked out totally! She began screaming and yelling. Swearing quite a lot at the CO (short for Correctional Officer) on duty.

Two other officers were called to the pod in an emergency escort to place this "crazy" women into her cell! Shortly after, one of her friends went to check on her because it had become very quiet in her friend's cell.

Well, the crazy women who had reported the lice case luckily didn't have any dental floss to harm herself with. She only had a plastic razor!

Cleverly, she had broken off the blue plastic casing and used the razors to slit her wrists!

She is the crazy one?

ALL THE COLORS and décor are like that of a dog kennel. That's it, a place that reminds me of where I used to drop off my dogs when we went away. Our dogs, however, probably got better treatment!

No ladder is provided to climb up into my top bunk. I have to hoist myself up by placing my right foot onto the bottom bunk and swinging my left leg up using my arms to help with the boost and to secure my body. My bunk is narrow, about two and half feet wide. Close quarters here, to fit as many of us as possible. The bunk has a mattress as hard as the floor. It is maybe two inches thick. Because of this, after days of incarceration, my body—thighs and legs mostly—is badly bruised.

The top sheet and the bottom sheet that I use to tuck myself in at night are a filthy gray hue. Maybe at one time they were white, but not anymore. The blanket is a rough, woolen lump, reddish brown in color. It reminds me of the blanket my daughter Kristen would put on her horse after a riding lesson. The pillow is flat and very hard, and also covered with a filthy gray pillowcase, to coordinate with the filthy gray sheets, of course!

The smell in here is the smell of nothing. Nothing is inviting.

Nothing is nurturing or hopeful. NOTHING!

The sights, the sounds and the smells all scream of a slow death to our souls. Our feelings of fear, guilt and shame are heightened. There is not one thing here to help us to start healing.

I LIE IN my top bunk to look out of the narrow window. It is four and a half inches wide by two foot high. Wonderful, I get the bunk with a view! The first cell I was in was in the center of the pod. Window free and shared with a young girl coming down off heroin. She was an addict who physically and mentally needed medical attention. She yelled and screamed a lot, when she wasn't puking her brains out for the first three days.

I was petrified; I had never been in trouble my whole life. It was beyond belief what was going on in here! I trembled with fear that she would become violent and take it out on me! I couldn't sleep or eat. My filthy gray pillowcase became tear stained as I wept, my cries unheard because of all the noise coming from our cell.

By the fourth day I was able to talk to her. She had been arrested and incarcerated several times for the same offence. It was incredible that just one of these experiences in jail, or prison, as she said she had been, wouldn't scare her straight! Trouble was, she was more dead than alive, merely existing.

A secured window, with a bar across the outside, obscures my already slim view even more. My new room faces Valley Street. I can see two, no, three red pine trees on this side of the street. I can tell they are red pines because of the long needles and the color of the bark on the tree. Science class served me well!

It's windy out. I can't hear the wind, but I can see the branches moving. The breeze does not caress my frail, bruised body, but I can remember how it felt.

Cars are passing by. Some people are driving all alone, and some cars have a driver and a passenger, and some have more.

One car, a white Volvo, has four passengers. It looks like a family. A mom, a dad, and two children in the back, going somewhere, someplace, together. That was me once, I think.

The cemetery is across the street. I can see the headstones inside the wrought iron fence. Different shaped headstones in rows. Mostly off-white in color, some gray and worn with age. Stones large and small marking the places where people have been laid to rest. They are all dead.

They cannot share their stories anymore. They cannot eat, drink, laugh, cry, work, play or pray anymore. They cannot be there for their friends, neighbors or family anymore.

I can, though. I almost couldn't. I almost took my life away, ended it all over LOVE. A dangerous, self-sacrificing love. Addictive Love.

My values, my dreams, my beliefs thrown to the wind.

EVERYTHING!

I never, ever imagined I would end up here in jail, but I did. Martin Luther King said, "Violence is a result of hopelessness and despair." The petrified, bruised, almost broken, cornered cat had finally, after years of holding back, fought back. Unfortunately, I did not use my sharpened claws to fight the fight, I used a weapon, a handgun.

A gun originally bought to kill myself. Suicidal, turned homicidal, in an evangelistic surge to prevent the predator from pouncing on any other unsuspecting, innocent prey.

And the Thunder Moon waned.

TWO

I WAS BORN on August 20, 1955 to Dolores Rioux (Bagwell), and Ernest Rioux. They had only known one another for a brief four months before marrying. Four months mind you, but they probably felt like it was REAL love, and were married in July of 1954.

My mom was only 19 years old when I arrived. She had just celebrated a birthday on August 11. My father used to tell me, "Your mother was beautiful. She had jet-black hair, real shiny, that fell to her shoulders. She had hazel eyes, big and bright, and an incredible smile and a nice figure." As he would share his description of her, his eyes would well up with tears. Sometimes the tears would run down his cheeks. He still carried a flicker of light for her.

Evidently, she loved to have fun. She did not like school, and never finished high school. From the stories my dad shared with me later on, my mom was out of high school more than she was in. I believe she only completed her freshman and sophomore years.

My grandparents did not speak of my mother. I learned about my mother from my father when I went to live with him when I was in the eighth grade.

I guess my grandparents tried to tame her, to understand her, but to no avail.

My mom, however, as I would find out from my counselor, Mr. K, who knew and had treated my mom–*how ironic!*–stated that she had been forced to eat a "Shit Sandwich," as he had put it, growing up in the Bagwell household.

There was a possible molestation that occurred when my mom was about five years old. I am not sure about the details. My mom brought it up in the car one day, as I was bringing her back to the state hospital, which she had called home since she was in her twenties.

When she told me, I was distraught, and overcome with raw emotion! Oh, how horrible. I could almost feel her pain. After I dropped her off, I drove slowly back to Manchester, tears streaming down onto my shirt.

"I am so very sorry, Mom," I said to myself. "You did not deserve what happened to you! I love you." I wished that I could have been there to stop it from happening.

The very next day, I asked my grandmother about it. She simply dismissed the subject, as she did all subjects too painful to discuss.

The secrets, and all the lies, the pure destruction of the events. It left behind ugly scars. Always denial that they had occurred! A double abuse, if you will. For not to address these things is like another violation!

There was drinking. A lot of drinking.

My grandfather, my mother's dad, was an alcoholic. Not a silly, fun loving drunk. Not a leave you alone, nowhere to be found drunk.

NO.

Unfortunately, when my grandfather drank, he became violent—a spinning out of control, abusive husband, father and grandfather. He had beaten up my grandmother often. My mother, Dolores, and her sisters Joan and Nancy had witnessed the horrors of his addiction more often than my brother Jim and I.

I believe he was probably extremely frustrated. Over-worked, with many pressures from his widowed mother and the nine siblings left behind. His mother was the main pain, from what I was told. You see her husband, my grandfather's dad, Mr. Bagwell, had died at the age of 43 of appendicitis.

Amazingly, no one had sat down and talked to me about any of this. I just listened intently when the liquor took over, and then all the dirty little secrets spilled out all over the floor like rainbow Skittles. It was the way I was educated about my colorful family history, one piece, Skittle, at a time. I knew deep down in my very soul that something was just not right! In fact, there were things that were terrifying and horrible, and I felt there had to be a reason.

In the Name of Love

The adults around me just couldn't be the way they were without a very good explanation. That is where faith comes in. The endless supply of unconditional love from the big guy, God, upstairs. The way I used to love everyone. Now, my soul tells me: NO!

MY GRANDFATHER'S FAMILY had ten children. My grandfather, James, was one of two sons born to the Bagwells . He had an older brother John, who had left home at the age of eighteen or so, (Hmmm...Smart boy), leaving behind my grandfather, James, to pick up all the jagged little pieces.

Bridget Bagwell, my grandfather's mother, was a very demanding woman, with an agenda of me, myself and I. Once again, hearsay, but with the behavior my grandfather exhibited, it now seems true.

I guess Bridget gave my grandfather regular speeches doused with her opinion on obligations to her and his six sisters, now that she was a widow, and his older brother John was gone. Well, to make a long story short, her guilt trip worked, and James was there to help his mother out at her every beck and call!

James had the responsibility of his own businesses: three local gas stations in Manchester, NH. He was also a husband to Margaret, his wife and the father to three daughters, Dolores (my mother), Joan, and Nancy, who was born later on. Along with the demands of a controlling mother, well, his plate was full.

I am not making any excuses for battering of any kind, verbal or physical. However, I am trying to understand what was going on, because I want ABUSE to stop! To end this destructive cycle in my family, because abuse is UNEXCEPTABLE!

I believe that, throughout our lives, the people around us have an enormous influence, and we can be led down certain paths because of them. Of course, that good old Catholic upbringing can do a number on you, as I can attest to! The church and its leaders were masters at leaving you with choking feelings of guilt, fear and shame. Justifying any action in the name of LOVE of others.

Yes, my grandfather was your classic example of codependency:

his suffering entwined with his mother and passed on to his children.

And so, my mother did not escape the clutches of fate. As a young child, Dolores and her sisters were subjected to all their father's fears and frustrations. He did not vent to the outside world, but instead would come home to vent, to take off his mask and share his darkness with his family.

My mom suffered from severe depression and mental illness, though she was not diagnosed as such until after the birth of my brother Jim. I do believe that sickness of any kind, mind or body, can be a product of the kind of environment that you are living in.

There were many red flags flying high prior to her collapse. Time can heal, but time can also destroy. I can vividly recall Aunt Joan saying, "Mary used to do strange things." What were these things? Childish whims, perhaps, that were misunderstood, or rather the acts of someone in desperate need of some professional attention. No one will ever know. I've only been able to glimpse tips of the iceburgs as I pass along in the ocean of this life. Whatever though, they did the best they could with what they knew.

THAT WAS MY mom. A childhood filled with lots of FEAR. She had seen and heard a lot by the time I arrived. There were lots of unresolved issues. How can you give the gift of LOVE when you don't have any to give to yourself? Then, you add the mental illness to that, and you have a recipe for a problem. A big problem! A disaster just waiting to happen, like the calm before the storm.

"I love you, Mom," I whisper to myself as I write the words in my journal, not wanting anyone to know I'm keeping one. They are not permitted here in jail. Sister Magarete, a good friend of the dean I had when I attended Notre Dame College, told me to keep one. She works here at the jail and has been instrumental in maintaining my sanity.

"I wish I could have been there to help you, Mom."

And the Thunder Moon waned.

THREE

MY FATHER, ERNEST, was born on April 9, 1926 in Augusta, Maine. His parents were Phillip and Alexandra, who were originally from Canada. They were living in Maine at the time when my dad was born because of the lack of work in Canada, therefore making my dad a citizen of the United States.

Soon after, when jobs had become more plentiful, my dad, along with his mother, father, an older brother, James, two younger brothers, Phillip and Jerad, and a sister (I don't remember her name) returned to Canada.

Dad had to deal with many hardships in his life. When he was six years old, a severe dairy allergy took the life of his only sister; she was just two years old. Then when he was eight, his beloved mother became a victim of TB. Leaving behind her four sons and her husband.

The youngest brother, Jerad, was placed with another family. Their father wasn't well, either. He suffered from a heart condition. Maybe his heart was broken due to the loss of his wife Alexandra and being left with four young boys. Soon after, their father's father, their Pepere, moved in to assist with the boys and all the daily tasks like cooking and maintaining their home.

So much sadness, so much pain at such a tender age, and he carried around his pain and the pain of his family too. He had embraced his past, as was evident whenever he shared the stories of his history with me. His voice would get shaky and tears would fill his eyes, emotions heightened by his large consumption of alcohol. He had not, however, learned how to MOVE BEYOND his past!

As I would listen to him attentively day in and day out, I would pray that I could make it all better for him, and in the name of love, I took on his pain.

In the Name of Love

WHEN I WAS thirteen years old, I went to live with my dad. Actually, it was just on the other side of the duplex my grandparents owned and lived in. I became my dad's counselor by the process of being his daughter, and living in the same house. Imagine, providing services when you don't even have a degree!

In some way, I am grateful that he shared his past with me, because although I cannot condone some of his behavior, I truly do understand it. His frugality came from a life of living in poverty. He and his family lived on welfare. His dad's illness prevented him from working. Dad said that they were given four dollars a week. FOUR dollars a week for a family of five! I believe that because my father had grown up under such conditions, he wanted to hold on to every penny, out of pure fear. I am sure that he did not want to ever return to a life lived in poverty again.

At the age of sixteen his father passed away, due to his failing heart condition. A few months later, his grandfather died too. Overcome with grief and sadness, I think that my dad felt all alone in the world, lost.

Where would he go? What would he do? He couldn't finish attending high school, and instead had to go to work so that he could provide himself with the basics of food and shelter. An auction was held to sell what little furnishings that they had, so that my dad and his brothers could pay for the funeral expenses and any other debts.

My dad and his three brothers said their good-byes and parted. Each going his separate way to find shelter from the storm of this life. My father told me of the great sense of abandonment he felt when he went back into the house the next day to find it completely empty. Nothing was left of the family that once lived there. It must have hit him like a thousand knives all over his body as he told me, "Kate, the auction took away not just the furniture, but my life as I knew it."

Every time he shared that story with me, I would cry along with him. He didn't cry with loud sobs, or make much noise. Instead, tears would just roll down his cheeks. For he had not let go of all the pain, and kept on embracing the pain of the past. He had never learned that he could let it go!

I felt all his pain too, and I wished with all my heart and my soul that I could have been there to do something. His grief became my grief, and at times I was overcome with guilt that I couldn't do anything to make it better for him. I now know that I couldn't have saved him, he had to save himself! But, in the name of LOVE of my dad, I listened again, again and again. Where was I going to go? There was no place to run to, or hide. I was thirteen, then fourteen, and so on, and that was my home.

Anyway, Dad went on to live in a boarding house. The house provided a roof over his head, warm meals, and some clothes, but not the love he needed. His heart remained empty.

My dad's foundation was built on sand, not rock or stone. Just like my mother, Dolores. I believe it was their insecurities that drew them together, like magnets. One trying so hard to please the other, both hoping that the other would FIX the foundation. Just to be loved no matter what! Looking, searching for the OUTSIDE cement.

And the Thunder Moon waned.

FOUR

DOLORES, ERNEST AND – soon after - Kathleen Rioux lived in Manchester, NH. I recall my father saying to me that our first home was on Conant St., on the west side of Manchester, near West High School.

IN THE SPRING of 1956 my mother became pregnant again. I was only nine months old at the time. Mom had just barely recovered from having me. (My own children were two years apart, and I cannot imagine having them any closer than that!)

I hope she was happy, but I never really knew. I think she was just trying to survive. Doing what she thought you were supposed to do.

In the fall of 1956, my father was told by the Air Force that he would be transferred to France. Due my mother's condition—pregnancy—the Air Force would not let her fly overseas with him.

So off to France he went to serve his country, leaving behind Dolores and I, with no choice in the matter. When the Air Force decided, it was carved in stone. How great was the impact of that decision on my mother's life, our lives as well? I will ever know.

Dolores then was forced to live with her parents, Margaret and James. I'm sure it was very hard to move back home. I just know it. I know my grandparents. The disappointment they would show, their frustrations, the "I told you so," all just waiting to be poured over her like tar and feathers.

I understand where my grandparents were coming from. I do. I really do. No judgment call.

My grandparents had not healed from their past.

They were living in FEAR not LOVE!

The cycle needs to end! Its time break the abuse and the

immaturity. Something more easily said than done.

And the Thunder Moon waned.

FIVE

ONE ELEVEN YOUNG St. was now a full house: James, the father; Margaret, the mother; Dolores, daughter and mom; Joan, the middle daughter; ten-year-old Nancy, the youngest daughter; fifteen month old ME, and a little brother or sister on the way. The living conditions must have been challenging. My mom probably felt like a bird flying for the first time with her newfound freedom, only to have her wings clipped off, and then be caged.

My father felt that something was wrong. He sensed that my mother was feeling very depressed from the few letters he had received from her while he was in France. He told me that the last few were not upbeat at all, and that she seemed very distraught and extremely unhappy.

On February 15, 1957, James Joseph Rioux entered into our world. A beautiful baby boy! He was the first boy in the family, and to my grandmother, a king. For I learnt early on, that there were two sets of rules in our Irish household: one set for the women, and another for the men.

I find it very interesting that the so called "Black Sheep" of the family, my mother, was the only female out of three others, my grandmother, Joan or Nancy, to produce a male.

Well, actually my mother had another boy, Raymond, from her boyfriend, Raymond Demers, in 1959 I believe. It was quite the scandal mixed with a dash of jealousy. Oh, Mom.

Imagine that, the troubled one was providing the world with such blessed gifts!

SHORTLY AFTER THE great joy, came the great sorrow. A few weeks after the birth of my brother my dad received an urgent message from his commander to report to the main office.

"Your wife has suffered a nervous breakdown, Ernest," said the commander. "You will be shipped home tomorrow, pack up your things and be prepared for your departure. Good Luck."

Ernest was overcome with many raw emotions. So horrified by the news, and not knowing what condition he would find his wife in upon his return to the states. He flew out the very next day on an emergency flight.

When Dad finally arrived back in Manchester, NH, he could not believe what he found! His beloved wife was totally beaten down, mentally and physically. All the pressures had been too much for her to deal with, just too much. Her parents, her siblings, a toddler, and a newborn were hard to cope with. Add to that the chemicals she had been given, swirling around inside her, and all her fears, well, they all won, I am so sorry to say.

"This was not the women I had left behind. No!" my father told me, his head hung down. "Kathy, your mom was never the same."

MY MOTHER was then brought to the State Hospital in Concord, NH, a mental institution. I believe she was suffering from post-partum depression, and instead of treatment, it seemed more like punishment! However, that is what they did to you in 1957. They gave you away to strangers, severely drugged you, gave you electro-shock therapy, then hoped that you would get better. What an atrocity, to say the very least, and what a terrible tragedy for a twenty-year-old woman.

Evidently, my grandmother was caring for my brother and I while Mom was recovering. My grandmother was around 45 years old at this time. She had finally gotten out of the house, had a job at the 724, a cigar factory located on Canal St. She really loved that job.

Margaret had made friends, and she was making money. She had tasted some freedom, and independence, and I'm sure it must have felt good, really good! Who knows what this newfound freedom would have led too? Who knows? She might have been able to free herself from her bondage.

In the Name of Love

~

OUR GRANDMOTHER agreed to take us in. The guilt, I believe, won over, washing over her like a cold shower— you're clean, but you just froze your ass off. She watched us for a couple months while Dolores was in the State Hospital recovering. Gram was anxious to get back to her job, however, to begin again. To finally be able to take time for Margaret, or "Peg," as her close friends referred to her, and with that frame of mind, understandably so, she wanted to return to the cigar factory.

AND SO MY mom was released from the State Hospital against the wishes of the doctors. They had stated that they felt my mother had not fully recovered. This was the beginning of the end for Mom, for my brother Jim and I, and for my dad. A domino effect of heartbreak, if you will, because we were attached to the idea of what a wife and mother should be.

My mom came and my grandmother went back to her job at the cigar factory.

MY DAD WAS now stationed at Grenier Air Force Base, here in Manchester, NH. It would allow him to be closer to my mother, Jimmy and I. For about nine months, a ritual of madness went on. Dad would leave for work and leave Jimmy and I in the care of our mother, who was not completely well.

So, just imagine: Dad would leave in the morning to go to work, and then come home at night. Often times he would find us unchanged, unfed and unattended. To think that this was allowed to continue for months, well, it makes me cry. My mother stopped talking to my father, and soon after, Dad said, "She started leaving on Friday nights and coming back early Saturday mornings." Mom had told my father that she wanted to work, and that she had gotten a job in a restaurant somewhere.

She lied.

In the Name of Love

She was seeing another man, Raymond Demers. No one knew about it, yet!

The lengths of her absences were becoming longer and longer. Friday's turned into Saturday mornings, then weekends, then weekdays. Something was definitely up!

What amazes me is how long my dad put up with my mom's behavior. I believe he was living in FEAR, not in LOVE. He was petrified to leave her, but he put all of us in jeopardy. Great danger in fact! I think he wanted to hold onto Dolores as long as he could. It seems like she was more like a possession, a trophy, if you will, and not a person.

And the Thunder Moon waned some more.

SIX

THE NEXT FEW years were filled with many moments of darkness. My mother had abandoned all of us for another man, and another family. You see, Raymond had three children of his own. Which cut even deeper, a man was one thing, but to leave my brother Jim and I to care for someone else's children seemed wrong.

My mother, however, had no desire to return to her past life. My father had done everything he could to get her back with him, with us. So my father had no other choice but to file for a legal separation. His Catholic beliefs were so strong at the time that he didn't file for divorce.

We lost both parents that day in court with the swift thud of the judge's gavel. They both checked out, but they weren't dead. Somehow, it's kind of worse when your parents leave you, and they are still alive.

The court awarded my grandparents, James and Margaret Bagwell, guardianship of my brother and I. Dad would continue on with his career in the Air Force. He would send money for our care, for food and clothing, to my grandparents. Then, he just went away; he hid. I believe it was all too painful. He was too overwhelmed to be able to care for us on a daily basis. I think we were a reminder of his life with her, Dolores.

Mom was now with Raymond Demers, pregnant with his child, and helping to raise his three other children. I remember her coming over to get her mail, with Raymond and his children in the car. I would run to the car to greet her, only to be ignored, as she headed toward the house to take care of her business there. She didn't even acknowledge me, but looked through me, like I was a ghost or something. My little heart was hurting, as I hoped for just a "Hello" from her. "You are my mother, I am here, I am here," I would say to myself, but she never said anything. Realizing that I wasn't getting anywhere with my mom, I would then approach the car, hoping to get a response from someone inside. I was curious about them, and in some way I wanted them to know who I was. We didn't even have to exchange words; just a wave would have been enough for my hopeful little heart.

Raymond, my mother's boyfriend, would force a "Hello." His three children, all girls, just sat in the deep back seat of the car, looking scared, staying still, for fear of letting anyone know that they were even there. It was behavior I knew so very well.

Be still my child or the storm might come.

ONE ELEVEN YOUNG St. offered some sense of stability, and security. My grandfather, up until this time, had been an abuser, and an alcoholic.

There, I said it! Heaven forbid I say it, family forbid that is, but it is the truth, and the truth does set you free!

Anyway, one of the positive effects of this tumultuous situation was that my grandparents became our guardians, an effect that closed the door, temporarily, of abuse on my grandmother, Margaret. My grandfather had promised to stop drinking if our grandmother would take care of us. No more drinking meant no more beatings. For James was mean and extremely violent when he drank. Like a raging typhoon hitting the inside of your home. Leaving you to find shelter any way you could.

It was a tradeoff, a deal. Good for Margaret Bagwell, my grandmother. Well, good for a little while at least.

SEVEN

MY RECOLLECTIONS OF that time are still pretty clear. The house we lived in was called a cape. It was brick red, with black shutters. Next door, to the right, was the home of Mr. and Mrs. Perkins, and their children. At that time, up until 1963, there was Carol, the oldest, Patty, who was my "BESTEST" friend and the same age as me, and Timothy, who was a few years younger than my brother Jim. There was a set of twins, Celia and Paul and another boy John who came later on. All in all, they had a complete packaged family of six kids. Wow!

Patty was my very best friend at that time. I can recall how wonderful she was to be with. In the summertime, when we were as free as birds from school, I fondly remember how we would begin our days. You see, Patty's bedroom was on the second floor of their light blue cape house, it faced east. My bedroom was also on the second floor—I am so glad I had graduated up there—and it faced west. Sweet, just perfect for early AM greetings done through open windows!

"Good morning Patty," I would yell out my window at the top of my lungs, if I was the first one to wake. I wonder now if I woke up anyone else in the neighborhood. No complaints as of yet.

"Good morning, Kathy," would be my early morning alarm clock, if Patty woke first.

These were the simple, carefree moments in my childhood.

Patty and I were inseparable, playing together as much as we could. Dolls, ball, going to Prouts Park, and so much more.

JEFFREY WALLACE WAS a boy who lived in the house just behind us. He was dear to me, too. Not quite as dear as Patty Perkins, but someone who added a different kind of pure delight to the day-to-day life of a young girl under the age of eight.

My grandfather used to get a big kick out of Jeffrey. Jeffrey liked to come over to our house and perform for us. We would all sit down in our small cape kitchen: Gram, Grampy, Jim and I, and become the live attentive audience. Then, Jeffrey would serenade us with his own special renditions of songs like, "The Bear Went Over the Mountain," and "Jesus Loves Me." All the songs he had learned in Sunday School.

Sadly, in the summer of 1973, Jeffrey Wallace committed suicide. I remember him in high school. He was a loner, and different. I remember when I heard about it, I cried. I hadn't talked to him in years, but even at that time there was something about suicide that I understood. I guess I cried because I wished I could have been there to stop him. He was only eighteen years old.

How much did he hate himself? How much had life beaten him up?

I know how much. I do. I understand why he did it. Thank you, Jeffrey Wallace, for the joy you brought!

EIGHT

MARGARET BAGWELL, MY grandmother, was there, but she wasn't. She seemed to me to be a very wounded woman, on the edge most of the time, in my presence anyway. Being around her was like you were walking on eggshells.

I can hardly blame you Gram, I do understand now, I do! I am not in judgment here. I am only trying to understand and be compassionate with the feelings I was having. And often times, I felt like I was a bother to her, but it wasn't my fault what happened. The choices she made were her own!

I distinctly remember being told to be very good, or I could be put in an orphanage. Little did the people that said that (and it wasn't just my grandmother) know that those words echoed over and over again in my little mind.

Behave, be good, or else! And I did.

YOUNG STREET WAS a tense place, and although there wasn't any verbal communication, there didn't have to be, because I could feel the tension. Feel it like a blast of arctic air. Like on a day when the thermometer goes below zero.

I am wired like that. To know what is going on by feeling it, ignoring all the warning signals to run or hide sometimes, instead, to stay, to help and yes, to save.

"It's all right. It's all right. They did not know any better," I would tell myself. "They didn't know better, and it wasn't me. They would have said or done those things to anyone," I'd say to myself for comfort. I had to learn acceptance, because I couldn't stop it!

In the Name of Love

AFTER MISS GEORGE'S kindergarten, I attended Our Lady of Perpetual Help. It was a Catholic grammar school where I went for first and second grade. Sr. Lucile, my second grade teacher, was a nun whose love and light provided us with a hide-a-key to unlock some of the chains of guilt and shame of Catholicism. We were lighter for a moment.

Down the street from us was Prouts Park. It was a neat playground with great equipment. Also, there was Paquette's Market, another refuge of sorts. An especially great place to get a popsicle on a hot, humid summer day. At Paquette's my Aunt Nancy and her friends would buy Coke in green 6oz. returnable bottles and Wise potato chips.

Yes, it seemed like a regular house, on a regular street, in a regular neighborhood, in a regular New England city. The family, well, they were secretly irregular. Excellent fakers, as were so many other families.

Then, for no real apparent reason, without even any notice, we were moving. Leaving!

OH, THE PAIN. The shattering of the friendships that had provided so much acceptance and joy to me, so much shelter from the storm of life.

Gram seemed so sad. She was so submissive to her husband, James, she had to go along with the move. Never, ever being able to voice her true opinion.

OUR NEW HOME was going to be at 6 Frontage Road, in the south end of Manchester. It seemed like a ride across the country to me at the time. And how in the world was I ever going to go on without Patty Perkins, my friend, my best friend. I was so overcome with emotion on the day that we moved. Good-bye seemed like such a terrible, horrible word, because I didn't want to go. I remember sobbing uncontrollably and trembling as I gave Patty one last hug before I had to leave, not wanting to let her go. Another loss that made my little heart ache so bad.

In the Name of Love

ABOUT A WEEK or so after our arrival to Frontage Road, I had the misfortune of coming down with an extremely bad case of Chicken Pox. YUCK! Maybe my mind was making my body react to my new home, and my heart missing my old home dreadfully. Jim was out and about at this time, while I slowly recovered. He was adventurous, exploring our new neighborhood. How I wished that I could have gone with him, joined him in his exploration. I just couldn't though, not yet anyway. I was "Contagious."

One day he arrived home after venturing down the street on his own, at the tender age of six; he came back all excited. He had met a girl that lived in our neighborhood. She was an older girl, about twelve, and her name was Elaine McGreevey. Jim had talked to Elaine, and found out that she had a sister that was the very same age as me! Her name was Judy.

I remember being very reluctant to meet Judy McGreevey. I was so afraid that she wouldn't be like my old friend Patty Perkins. Well, we finally did meet in the summer of 1963, lucky for me! For little did I know how much our friendship would mean in the years to come. You see, she saved me with her LOVE, with her understanding, her kindness and thoughtfulness, and with a warm and wonderful smile too.

Anyway, we did get along, fine, just fine and still do. We have shared some wonderful moments and times, and I cherish the memories. In the name of love of Judy, I was learning to love myself again.

And the Thunder Moon waxed.

NINE

TODAY IS THE 2nd of February, 2002. Little did I know that I, Kathleen Rioux would be here. Not so much here, as in Gary Tardie's apartment typing a story—an incredible story, my story, one of profound learning, earth shattering, tidal waving, skin crawling kind of experience—but here as in my life, picking up the shattered pieces of hope. And going to a place I guess I needed to go to, all IN THE NAME OF LOVE.

JUDY MCGREEVEY AND I went to St, Francis of Assissi School. In 1963 we entered into the third grade. Sister Valley was our teacher, I believe. It was there at St. Francis that I also met Leslie Brewster. Two wonderful women, now, and the three of us were so compatible. Funny thing is, to this day we still are!

Third grade was a year filled with following rules and regulations. The nuns certainly knew how to keep you in line. Fear and humiliation were their tools. They worked well, very well. Being submissive was encouraged and remaining QUIET was a good thing. We couldn't even talk at lunchtime.

The oppression imposed on us still, to this day, rears its ugly head. I'm not holding all of the Catholic religious population responsible, just some of them. Submissive behavior was encouraged, and better yet, even honored. Which, I believe, is the main reason the sexual abuse of so many innocent children went on for so long, silenced by fear.

Once, when I was in first grade and was talking in line, I was smashed across the face. The nun slapped me so hard that it took my breath away. On another occasion, when I was in the fifth grade, I was strapped for talking at lunchtime. I refused to cry in fifth grade, I didn't want to give Sr. Francis, the principal, the satisfaction of thinking she had silenced me. And she didn't, for here I write.

Standing up for oneself is critical, essential for our very survival. For even the creatures of the wild are taught to protect themselves from predators. And it all begins with each one of us. The respect, the love, it starts with you!

THINGS AT HOME were becoming clearer now. I certainly had learned now to play my role very well. Actually, they say by the time you are about three, you know how to survive in your home life. I wanted so desperately to be loved and accepted, the tension always seemed to be there, eggshells everywhere I walked. The adults around me at any given moment set the tone, mostly my grandfather James and then my grandmother, Margaret, when my grandfather wasn't around.

Then there was my dad, a passer-by, an infrequent flyer. Who could only stay, on his spur of the moment visits, until the sun began to set, telling us that he couldn't drive in the dark.

Oh, the irony of it all, as time and place would tell all later on.

GRAMP HAD GIVEN up alcohol for about ten years or so. However, for some reason he opened up that Pandora's Box, and the drinking started again. Unleashing his pent-up anger, frustrations and abuse.

I'm not sure what exactly triggered it, as children we weren't given much information. Although, I don't know what good it would have been for me to know why he drank back then. I was about nine when my innocence was stripped away, leaving the horror of my grandfather's drinking to show itself in living color. My brother Jim was only seven.

James Bagwell could be so attentive at times, even fun loving! I fondly remember times of singing in the car as we drove to the beach, one of Grampy's favorite places. Playing catch in the backyard of Frontage Road, or going for ice cream on a hot summer night to Glendens on Second Street, right here in Manchester.

Yes, there were some good times, even great moments. Like when Grampy would take us onto the beach to explore. Hunting for treasures that the high tide would bring in: a starfish, a snail, or maybe, just maybe, a crab. Oh, when Grampy was in a good mood, the world was a wonderful place to be!

The bad times, however, were very, very bad. So scary. Once that anger switch flipped on, often times without any warning, like a tornado, it would trigger such rage that I was petrified of him. All the great moments would be washed out to sea with the tide. There were times when he was so violent that we would have to quickly pack up and go to my Aunt Joan's. He would totally unravel, yelling and throwing things around.

I remember just turning myself off. Literally, I couldn't hear anything, I couldn't feel anything, and I couldn't say anything.

Nothing.

I froze myself. I would thaw out later when there was more room in my subconscious mind.

In the name of love for my grandfather, I would only focus on all the "Good" things he had done as I cowered on my bedroom floor, curled up in a fetal position, praying and waiting for the tornado to end.

If we had to run, we would return the next day to our house on Frontage Road as if nothing had ever happened. It was like having an elephant in your living room, sitting on your couch, and no one saying anything about it!

MY MOTHER HAD RETURNED to the mental hospital.

My grandfather told us that we must visit our mother; that it would be good for her. Traumatic for us, but good for her.

So, we would wait on this big couch, Jim and I, our legs too short to touch the floor, dangling over the edge, as I recall my earliest memories of our visits. Wait for one of the staff members, nurses I presume, who were dressed in starched white uniforms, with matching cupcake shaped hats on their heads, to fetch our mom.

She seemed like a caged animal in a kennel, as she would appear from a locked door, a door with a screen covering the place where a window should have been. I remember vividly, the sterile staff, like the head nurse in *One Flew Over the Cuckoo's Nest*, bringing our mother, Dolores, over to the couch where Jim and I were sitting. She was in a daze most of the time. Drugged up for sure.

Grampy Bagwell would say to my mom, "Here they are Dolores. Here's Kathy and Jim. Your daughter and son."

I would anxiously wait for her to respond to us. I would pray silently to God and say to myself, "Just say something mom. A smile would be nice, or a hello, a gentle pat, a handshake, or maybe, just maybe, a hug. Oh, how wonderful that would be. Once you hold us, Mom, you'll wake up from your frozen state and see how good we are."

I would finish my silent prayer with, "You'll get better, and you'll come home and be our mother. We want you Mom. Mom, Mom, MOM," my little voice inside would scream.

Nothing would happen, though. My mother would just stare off into space. No response, not even a nod. So lifeless; this was my mother.

The visits weren't very frequent, thank god, maybe two or three times a year, usually around the holidays, and on my mom's birthday in August. I was so glad that my mother had a summer birthday, because then we could take her to the ocean. Mom loved Hampton Beach. To be able to splash in the salty water gave her such joy, and it made me happy to see her smile and laugh for a moment. After our trip to the beach we would finish our day with a stop at an ice cream stand. Mom liked ice cream, too!

For some reason, I could feel her pain. She didn't even have to talk to me, but I knew that she was hurting badly inside. I saw it in her eyes, the window to her soul, though I didn't know just yet by whom, or by what, she had been hurt.

Sometimes my mother would go in without a fuss. Other times she would plead with my grandfather to let her come home. I could hear her sobbing and begging him, "Please let me come home, Daddy. Please, I'll be good."

"No, you can't come home Dolores. You're not ready," my grandfather would say, as he took her by the arm and escorted her back to the large red brick building. I would turn around and look out the rear window of the car, and I would cry in silence, not daring to make a sound. Warm, salty tears would roll slowly down my cheeks. "I love you so much mom. You'll get better someday," I would tell myself. "I will pray for you, and I will be a good little girl so that you'll love me."

And so, the truths of my mother were slowly being discovered. Little by little, I would overhear bits and pieces of information about her. I was starving for her truth. Someday, everything would fall into place. However, being eight or nine leaves you with a strong willingness to hold onto childhood, and many things were just stored way back in my subconscious, only to rear their ugly head later on.

And the Thunder Moon waned.

TEN

IN THE SUMMER of 1967, Judy McGrevey and I were walking down Kemberma Hill. I don't recall where we were headed at the time, most likely to Red's Market for some ice cream or a popsicle. Anyway, we ran into some boys. One of them was Douglas, and the other Billy.

Our hormones were just starting to kick in then, so seeing them sparked some interest and curiosity. A year earlier we would have said, "Yuck, boys" and ran; but this time not so much.

They said "HELLO" really loud from the bottom of the hill. Then they asked, "Hey, do you girls want to make out?"

We didn't respond immediately, we needed to think about this one. "What does 'Make Out' mean, Judy?" I asked innocently. We didn't even have a clue. So, being two naïve little Catholic girls, we asked, "What does make out mean?"

In unison they quickly responded, "It means to KISS!" We were a little confused! They wanted to kiss us? Why?"

However, our adventurous gene surfaced, and all of a sudden it sounded exciting! For up until that moment, I had only kissed family members and close friends.

So, we agreed on going into the nearby woods that ran along Kemberma Hill to KISS these boys.

It was an awkward moment in time, a turning point that I will always remember. Crossing over the threshold from childhood innocence to adolescence, into the great big wide world of choices.

In 1967 my world was on Frontage Road. The hormones were kicking in, and along with puberty came lots of feelings that were heightened. I began to feel things at a much deeper level, and I became sensitive to the words and the actions of all the adults around me.

It was also the summer that I learned that my father was an

alcoholic. Nobody had come out and told me to my face, but the day I realized it, my world changed for a long time.

I HAD BEEN sick with a stomach ailment; I had been throwing up for days. The strange thing about vomiting this time, was that it actually felt good. It got rid of a lot, especially food. Food, now that was something I could control. What to take in, what to keep, and what to lose!

I was twelve years old when I became anorexic. This precious, confused little girl, trying to survive in all the madness somehow. My last hope of being "Normal" was now shattered into a billion pieces. My dad had a drinking problem just like my grandparents. My last hope was hopeless.

The beginning of seventh grade was pretty much a blur. With the onset of puberty, the dysfunction of my home life, and now, the startling news of my father, it was all far too much for me to handle. My dying inside was showing up on the outside now.

In the fall of 1967 I was in and out of doctors' offices. None of them knew why I was losing weight. At my lowest, I weighed a slight 54 pounds. A battery of tests was done to me, some of them were disgusting, and humiliating as well. Like the Barium Enemas, and drinking a thick chalky liquid down. Then you stand in front of an x-ray machine while the liquid passes through your body. It actually lights up your insides! Then, the camera takes pictures to see what's going on.

I was hoping secretly that the doctors would find something physically wrong, then they could just give me some medicine, and all the painful past would just disappear. But, the pain I suffered from was locked up inside me. There were years of fear, misunderstandings, confusion and abandonment. I felt like I was a bother. I didn't know at the time that my family's issues were not my issues. I was too young. I was simply stuck in the mess of all the adults around me, a victim of circumstance.

I am not blaming the adults around me. I am not. I am just trying to understand their ways of survival, and not understanding why they did the things they did.

They were looking outside for the answers, not within themselves.

They did not know any better.

They did the best they could with what they knew.

IN THE SPRING of 1968, I was admitted to Boston Children's Hospital, in Massachusetts, for anorexia nervosa.

I was down to skin and bones, corpse-like, committing a slow suicide unconsciously. This young precious package. My dad told me years later that when I was taken to the hospital, they told him that I had only twenty-four hours to live.

In a way, going to the hospital far away from home was a godsend, it really was! I didn't have to deal with anybody's issues, just Kathleen's. I was relieved that someone knew what I needed. That was Dr. Jalbert, and he thought it would be better that I go to a hospital.

Thank you, Dr. Jalbert, wherever you may be. You saved me from all the people around me. For the first time I felt a crumb of freedom. Deep in my very soul, FREE! Scared to death, but free, nonetheless.

I continued to starve myself, but not as much. They would weigh my skeletal body every day. I would try to vomit whenever I could. Some food stayed down because I allowed it. Now though, deep down inside, I really didn't want to die. I wanted to live! I wanted someone to love me but, as I would find out later, that person had to be me.

I WAS A patient of the Boston's Children's Hospital from April 1968 until June of 1968.

The nurses were outdated, and definitely had no clue as to what my illness was all about. It was kind of a good thing in a way. They treated me as if I had some kind of physical ailment. Not a mental condition. To think that I might somehow be like my mother, at that time, would have been quite devastating to me!

I had held everything in. I didn't even know what the problem was sometimes. I had learned to just shut down; denial was easier. If I had faced all the drama then, I would have been blown away.

And the Thunder Moon waned.

ELEVEN

IT WAS IN June of 1968 that I plotted my getaway from Boston Children's Hospital. I'd had it with the place. My time there was done. I was back on my size 5 feet. I didn't care what the doctors said. I was as good as I was going to get. My eating disorder was under my control, not theirs, and I was in charge of me! I loved me, a little more than when I came. I would never last here. It was time to go!

My grandmother had been giving me money to make telephone calls. However, whenever I would call home, I would call collect, and keep the money.

You see, my grandmother would come to see me all the way from Manchester, NH by bus. I can only know the value of that trek as I sit here now. That she cared for me, and how brave she really was.

Thank you for coming Grammy, thank you.

Well, that sparked something in that little mind of mine. If my grandmother, Mrs. Bagwell, came and went by bus, then I could do the very same thing!

So, without any hesitation, I set out. I had never been in the city of Boston alone before, but when you become fearless, you are one with the universe, and anything is possible!

I had written in my diary the night before, "Dear Flower, (my diary's name) Today is my last day here! I need to go home. I will not spend another day in this terrible place!"

This was the first time in my life that I felt some control over my destiny. The adults all seemed like they didn't really care. Or better yet, they seemed numb. In more ways than one, I was in the driver's seat, and it felt so damn empowering. I was alive, and I wanted to be!

I know if I had stayed at Bostons Children's Hospital that I would have died for sure. I would have worn the hat. The label, if you will, of, ANOREXIC, and BULIMIC, which I was NOT! They were the symptoms of all the trauma, they were not me!

So, bag and baggage, I waited until the coast was clear, and headed for the front door of the building. When I got to the door, my heart was pounding so hard. But, I just took some deep breaths, went against my fears, and walked out calm and cool. I even waved good-bye to the secretary at the door.

Once out, I moved slowly at first, then little by little, I increased my pace. My walk turning into a run. There was no turning back now. I needed to get away from this place. This horrible place that made me feel bad about myself. Yes, at the time I was admitted, it was necessary. Walls can be a way of providing protection, regrouping and healing, as the hospital did. Now, their time was up, my twelve-year-old mind had decided. I had had enough. Quite enough, it was time to go HOME.

I ARRIVED IN Manchester, NH sometime in the evening. There was only one bus left for that day that could transport me to south Manchester, so I quickly boarded it.

I recall having this overwhelming feeling of empowerment, that I would be staying home, that I was much better. Well, still a work in progress, recovering every day. I was still Kathleen. Not anorexic, I was Kathleen, just a child who wanted so desperately to be loved. I guess I must have loved myself a little, because I saved myself. Nobody else could. I would make it, I had to!

When I arrived home, the tension was thick enough to cut with a knife. You would have thought that I was a hardened criminal! (That would come eventually).

My grandmother was irate. Her words were like pouring vinegar into a wound, burning and stinging, as she told me, "You had better eat something." Like the whole illness could be magically cured with FOOD, or the lack of it.

I did though.

I didn't care, I had to follow this command. If eating was a way of staying, then so be it. I ate that ham on white, with a dollop of mustard that my grandmother had placed in front of me. Chewed it slowly, and washed it down with some cold creamy milk. I forced myself to keep it down. I had to prove that I was "All Better."

I was, mostly.

MY GRANDPARENTS HAD called my father to let him know that I had arrived at the house on Frontage Road. I guess his first response was, "How did she get there?"

Another call was made by my grandmother, this time to Boston Police Department. They were notified of my arrival too! I was a minor who was missing, so they were on alert for me. The hospital had called back shortly after Gram had called them. The Children's Hospital was demanding that I be brought back that evening. It was my grandfather, James, thank God for him, who said, "No, Kathy stays here! If she had to take a bus to come home, then that hospital must be pretty bad."

Luckily for me, my grandfather had the power, and when he spoke, everyone listened. This time his power worked in my favor. Great for Kathleen Ann!

Jim, my brother, welcomed me with open arms. I sat on the edge of his bed and talked to him until I was summoned to go to bed. His room was a haven in that moment, for the frigid blast from my grandmother's eyes was more than I could bear. She was livid that I was there.

Dr. Jalbert, my pediatrician from Manchester, had called our home and recognized my desperate attempt to be in a different place than where I was. He told my grandmother over the phone that, "If Kathy is unhappy there, and has made such a move, then keep her at home."

As my grandmother, in a whisper, repeated verbatim to my grandfather what Dr. Jalbert had just said, I was in my bedroom listening. I said to myself, "Someone is supporting me." I had value, and I knew what I was doing!

THE SUMMER OF 1968 was a time of great growth for all. People like Dr. Vervon, a local psychiatrist in Manchester, NH, told me that the reason I was suffering from anorexia was definitely due to my situation at home. This was a most profound moment: *it wasn't me.* Imagine that, I had thought it was my fault all along.

Finally, things began to spill out of me. Some family members were outraged with my sharing, the skeletons weren't dancing. They were upset, angry, and deeply saddened, all because I was telling the truth. That is what it felt like most of the time.

That was the first layer of the crap sandwich that began to dissolve. Slowly, oh so slowly. It was twelve years of survival techniques I had to rid myself of, and to know that someone now knew it wasn't my fault gave me such a great sense of relief!

SUMMER TURNED INTO fall, and eighth grade began. The anorexia had turned into bulimia at this point, at the tender age of thirteen. At least I was allowing some of the food to stay with me. Most days were a blur, and I barely had enough energy to go to school.

My mind was consumed with ideas of walking home from our bus stop, which was probably about a half mile from our house, with as many of my books as possible, the heavier the bag the better. That meant more calories would burn, burn, burn.

Also, the idea of starvation seemed worse than binging and purging. I felt more in control, and what I didn't know at the time was that the extreme exercising I was doing actually helped me to cope with all the drama in my home. I was trying to create a balance somehow, and although I was very sick, I never gave up.

Somehow, I would dig down deep inside and pull myself up, just when it seemed like there was absolutely nothing left!

IN JANUARY OF 1969 my dad retired from the Air Force. I was somewhat ill-prepared for the storm that lay ahead. I had, however, become an accomplished eavesdropper, and the skill had somehow equipped me with the information I needed to survive.

For, if you listened carefully, you knew what was coming. It gave you a chance to RUN and HIDE! It was my plastic sword. My brother Jim and I hadn't been given any information on our father. We only knew what we learned about him from his infrequent visits: that he liked to chew Wrigley's Spearmint Gum, that he didn't smoke, that he could do 25 push-ups all at once, and when he flexed his biceps for us, we truly thought that he was our own personal Superman.

My grandparents owned a duplex. When we moved there in 1963, my grandparents and my brother and I lived on the side to the left when you were facing Frontage Road. The other side was rented out. The apartment on the other side, however, had been vacant for months before my father was to be discharged from the Air Force. Little did I know at the time, but the delay in renting the other apartment was in fact, intentional. Grampy really didn't want us to move away. He thought it better that we stayed next to them. Good call!

So, my brother Jim, my father and I moved into the vacant apartment on the other side of the house. We went to Falon's Furniture Store and furnished the kitchen, a lovely maple round table with four chairs. The living room, with a couch, two matching slightly stuffed chairs, a maple coffee table—believe me the table never had a cup of coffee on it—and two end tables that matched the coffee table.

The bedrooms were furnished with beds, dressers, and night stands. I was so excited, because for the first time in my life, I had my very own bedroom. I even got to pick out the bedroom set that I wanted. I selected a beautiful white provincial set. It came complete with a double bed, a dresser, a mirror and a nightstand.

WOW! Mine, all mine!

Jim and my dad shared a bedroom. My dad had furnished their room with a maple bedroom set. It came with two twin beds, a nightstand and two dressers, a tall one and a short one. The shorter one belonged to Jim so that he could have a place for his clothes and things. All the furniture, however, did not remove the anxiety that I felt deep down to the depths of my thirteen-year-old soul. Something was coming, something big.

Hush now. Hush now. Love your daddy, no matter what. Love your brother, no matter what. Love Grammy and Grampy, too. The message drilled into me through my Catholicism had saturated most of my mind. Be a good little girl.

So I was, in the name of love.

THE FIRST FEW WEEKS living with my father went pretty well. Ernest Rioux was on his best behavior, his visiting behavior. Which was polite, tolerant and cheerful, just like good old Dad. Then, one evening he didn't return home from work. My grandparent's reactions were not as I expected. They did not seem alarmed as they said rather calmly, "He'll be home soon."

Their words comforted briefly up until the early evening hours. After around 10pm or so my brother and I became frantic! Worry was devouring us like a ravenous grizzly bear. So many unanswered questions took over our thoughts. Where was he? Where could he be? The not knowing was so devastating. We waited and wondered, and could never calm ourselves. A sleepless night followed.

My father hadn't even bothered to call.

The next morning I was in a zone, but I still had to go to school. To carry on as if none of it had ever happened. The last bit of innocence stolen from me, and with the last thread of hope I thought to myself, "When I get home he'll be home."

It was one of the longest days of my life. The unknown and all that goes along with worry. I barely functioned through all my subjects, and Sister Margaret Agnes was of no help. I was running on empty, sleep deprived and unfed. How could she possibly expect me to answer math questions? It wasn't her fault; she had no idea what was going on behind closed doors.

I'll never forget when I was in eighth grade, Sister Margaret Agnes took me aside. It was time for morning recess, and she told me to wait in my seat. Once all the class had filed out, she came over to my desk.

I was in one of my worst states physically and emotionally, and now you could add a nervous wreck to the menu.

"You are killing your grandmother, you know, with what you are doing." Her words stung, just as if she had smashed me across the face. Of course, I did not respond. She was a nun, she was close to God. Therefore, she must be right. I simply lowered my head and nodded.

Sister Margaret was referring to the severe anorexia that I was suffering from. She just added another large dose of guilt and shame to my already overflowing cup. I was killing my grandmother. I was killing her!

SO, LIFE WENT on. I got what I wished for. I was with my father. I got to be a real live homemaker: cooking, cleaning, grocery shopping, and taking care of my dad and my brother, Jim at times. The good little girl, the thirteen year old who was to carry on the duties of an adult!

The next time my dad went off on a drinking binge, as I recall, it was close to the holidays. There was no Christmas tree on our side of the duplex. There were no presents. The truth was that none of that even mattered to me. I just wanted my dad to come through the door. To hold me in his arms and tell me everything was all right. That he had been captured by the enemy and he had tried to call, but they wouldn't let him! Finally, he was able to escape and come home to Jim and I as soon as he could.

There was a real enemy, it was the alcohol, but Dad had to free himself!

He never did.

THE THERAPY FOR the anorexia ended in my sophomore year of high school. I had convinced my counselor that I was fine. I had gained enough weight to warrant the notion that I was ready for the world.

High school was a most reflective time. I remained a good student, doing my assignments and trying to keep my grades up. I tried to make the honor roll. At that time, I equated making the honor roll with my value, my worth. Looking, searching outside myself so that my family would find me important enough to love.

It amazes me how focused I was then, so determined to remain true to my beliefs at that time. I was so conservative that I didn't date. Boys, well, *you know what they want* I had been told, and they were not getting it from me!

I HAD ALWAYS been spiritual for as long as I could remember. At an early age, say around 4 or 5, I came to the realization that the adult human beings around me were not reliable. I had an overwhelming sense of God's presence. I had a knowing that God would always be there for me. Up until I became an adulteress, I believed.

When I was a sophomore in high school my spirituality deepened, and it seemed to guide me to the Precious Blood Monastery. Whenever there was a death, or someone was very ill, my grandmother would go to get a mass card or light a candle in the chapel. It was an order of cloistered nuns who ran the monastery. It was so peaceful there, and when the nuns spoke to you, they seemed liked angels, like heaven on earth.

At fifteen I was extremely impressionable and religious. Becoming a cloistered nun, with no contact with the outside world, was an attractive lifestyle to me for two reasons.

First, the cloistered nuns always seemed calm, gentle and attentive. And the monastery they lived in was quiet, peaceful, orderly and filled with serenity. Quite a contrast to the drama-laden environment I came from. Contact with the nuns had always made me feel safe, like nothing could hurt me.

Second, my Catholic upbringing had demanded obedience, and encouraged sacrifice and martyrdom. Surely becoming a cloistered nun would please the nuns who taught me, my family and God. I would be loved more.

Luckily for me, the Mistress of Novices sensed my desperation to escape my home life, to run and hide away there. I referred to my feelings as a "Calling," but she gently explained that this would be a commitment to a lifetime of service, to compliance. She said that she saw in me someone who was adventurous and had a free spirit inside. And that eventually I would feel like a caged animal, who really needed to be free!

That, given the essence of Kathleen, this life would become a punishment used to escape my past. I was very disappointed of course. I was too young to face the truth then. I was just beginning to know myself.

But to this day, I am so grateful she set me free!

SOMETIME AROUND JUNIOR year in high school, we needed to go to the school nurse for physicals. Mrs. Roukey was the nurse in charge of the task of making sure our student bodies were healthy.

It was my turn to make a visit to Mrs. Roukey for my check-up. I really wasn't very keen on the idea because I knew it meant getting on a scale. For the anorexic (and I was still caught in its grip), scales are extremely frightening, dangerous tools. It's a way to measure how much of you is left here on this earth, and that is something that you want to keep hidden.

You pretend that you don't want to be noticed, but skeletons do not go unnoticed, and really, deep down inside I was screaming, "Please help me! Save me from the torment of my home life."

I weighed in at about 89 pounds. Self-inflicted? I don't think so! Environment inflicted, for sure.

Mrs. Roukey was very concerned. She took some time to talk to me. There was not even a dash of the shame spice, just genuine concern of how she could help.

We came up with a game plan of getting me a free meal ticket so I could get some lunch, and that she wasn't going to contact my dad, as long as I started to gain some weight. If I didn't, she would have no choice but to call a local doctor and report her findings.

So, in the name of Mrs. Roukey's concern for me, I complied.

In the Name of Love

THE ADULTS AROUND continued in their nightly binges, as did my anorexia and bulimia. I was so weak, just existing, as they were. I did not realize it at the time, but I was committing my own little death sentence, a slow suicide of sorts. Being able to control something, namely food, as I was slowly withering away, making Kathleen become extinct.

Every day for my grandmother, my grandfather and my father was a cause for drinking. It was no longer saved for festive occasions like Christmas or New Year's Eve, which had been hard enough to endure. Almost everyone ending up with slurred speech, unsteady balance, and then came the yelling, screaming and fighting.

When we would go out to restaurants, my grandmother would call out a cocktail order to the waitress even before she had her coat off. She would get so drunk at times, that she would get very loud. It seemed like just about everyone in the restaurant would be looking at us. Gram would order Manhattans "straight up," and the dread of what would follow was so painful. My grandfather wouldn't do anything. He would have a couple of "seven and sevens," but his tolerance for liquor was greater, so two drinks hardly affected him. Then, Gram would be wasted, and we would have to just about carry her out. It was so humiliating. It felt, once again, like they were the children and I had to step up and be the adult!

The homestead continued to be a painful place. I dreaded walking in the door, because you never knew what you would stumble upon. Gram had resorted to nightly drinking now. Drinking until she could barely make it to her room at the end of the day to retire. My grandfather would join her, and if they had beer, the mood would be mellow. But it the hard stuff was broken into, my he would become crazy!

So, once again the show had begun, the stage had been set with beer, wine or whatever alcoholic beverage that was available. It really didn't matter. The music in the background would elicit the happy emotions for the cast of characters in the opening act. The closing act would end in anger, betrayal and unresolved issues from the past.

In the Name of Love

THERE WAS A story told to me many times by my grandmother, Margaret, when she was no longer sober, when the alcohol had almost covered up the tip of the iceberg of pain. She would take her package of Marlboro cigarettes, open the flip top, and slide a cigarette out. The flip top would be closed and placed back on the table, as the cigarette dangled out, lightly held between her two lips. She would reach for the ash tray, and draw it over close enough to her so she would be able to easily flick her ashes into the ash tray, once the cigarette was lit. Then, she would reach for the matchbook, open it, and take a match out, close the cover, then strike the match against the sulfur flint on the cover. The used matchstick was immediately discarded into the ash tray.

"When I was nine years old," she would begin, "I was expected to come home and get dinner ready." The first thing she had to do when she came home from school was to start a fire in wood stove. Gram had to get the kindling wood, which was kept in a box by the stove.

Well, Gram, little nine-year old Margaret, had carefully placed some of the kindling into the stove, leaving some pieces of wood remaining in the box. She then lit the wood in the stove. Somehow, the match slipped out of her tiny hand, and found its way into the wooden box on the floor with the left-over pieces of wood. The box of wood on the floor caught fire and began to spread!

Being the smart nine year old that she was, fear warned her to act quickly, and she ran. Ran clear down from the third floor to the street. In the meantime, someone had called the fire department to come to put out the fire. Margaret had made it out safely! The neighborhood had been aroused with curiosity, and soon people were pouring out of their homes and into the street to see what all the commotion was about.

There she was, this little child, outside all alone. Probably trying to somehow comfort herself as best she could.

"I could hardly breathe, and my heart was beating wildly. Luckily I had escaped the clutches of the fire!"

In the Name of Love

The firemen were inside the apartment building, on the third floor, where my grandmother and her family lived, when Gram's mom arrived on the scene. Everything was under control. There had been a little damage to the kitchen floor, by the stove, and the box that held the kindling wood definitely needed to be replaced. Instead of being ecstatic that little Margaret was alive and safe and sound, Delia was furious! And the glare that she gave Gram as she came toward her confirmed it. A rage that seemed worse than the fire that the firemen were putting out.

Where were those firemen when you need them? I bet Gram wanted to yell, "Fire, Fire," as her mother parted through the onlookers. "Please, someone save me," she thought, as she stiffened up, trying to prepare herself for what was about to happen, because Gram knew one way or another she was going to get burnt too!

Well Gram's mother didn't waste a moment. She grabbed her by the arm abruptly, and began to spank her backside hard. Delia was outraged that my grandmother had started a fire and that "Now dinner was not going to be ready."

As my Gram told the story, each time I felt her heartache. Her mother's words and reactions to this accident said to her that the dinner not being made was more important than she was. And there she was, this grown women still hoping for a mother's love that never came. Emotionally, it seemed at times, she was still only nine.

I saw little Margaret, and I loved her.

So, in the name of love, my Gram took her punishment. She had failed to please her mother. She took on all her mother's pain. She felt unloved, unworthy, and she forever carried that message with her until the day she died.

Her mother's issues became hers.

There were other stories too. However, this one was told by my grandmother over and over again. It became etched on my brain. Then, Gram would start to sob, and the tears would roll down her cheeks and she would become that little girl again. The slurred speech and her unsteadiness made her seem even more childlike. That nine year old that wanted so desperately to be treasured.

I felt so useless that I couldn't save her, or help her. What was wrong with me?

And the Thunder Moon waned.

TWELVE

SO THE DANCE of passing down the torch of guilt, shame and fear continued. I took it on and carried it. I didn't really have a choice. My family gave me things I didn't ask for. They gave me the coping mechanism of just stuffing all your feelings and emotions, just take it, and don't tell.

Trouble is, I remember it ALL!

This story is not one to elicit your pity, mind you. Oh no! It is a way for me to get back my life, the one I was supposed to live, a life to be lived in LOVE, not in FEAR.

BACK IN THE late sixties, my dad decided that we would venture up to Montreal, Canada to meet his two brothers—Joseph his older brother, and Henry his younger brother—and all our cousins, whom we had never met yet. I was very excited about the trip. The chance to meet relatives from my father's side of the family seemed like such a wonderful idea. To travel far away from here, an even better one!

Finally, we arrived, and our Uncle Henry welcomed us with open arms. He was so happy to see us. I could feel the warmth in the air. When we went into his apartment he gave us a great big hug, and immediately wanted to know if we needed something to eat or drink. Such a sincere gesture of hospitality was so surprising, foreign even.

SOON AFTER BREAKFAST the next day, a good old Canadian Ale, the name I do not recall, was cracked open, the familiar sound echoing into the depth of my very soul. Loud and clear, it told me what the future would be bringing. Uncle Henry's girlfriend showed up shortly after, around noon, and the festivities were in full swing. The noise level, and the drinking, had increased greatly, as the threesome became a foursome when another male friend stopped by.

Let the celebration begin.

As the party continued on into the night, my brother Jim and I were getting hungry. My father, at this point, was drunk out of his mind. He couldn't even speak or walk across the room. We told Uncle Henry that we needed to eat something, and he was sober enough to comprehend what we were asking for. Then, he gave us some money to walk to the grocery store down the street. With slurred speech, Uncle Henry told us to go buy a package of hot dogs and some rolls. Then he proceeded to instruct us where we would find the store. Not one adult was able to drive us, or even walk with us, in a new country, to a grocery store we had never been to in our lives.

So, off we went out into the streets of Montreal to find the store. It was a few blocks away from Uncle Henry's apartment, and it actually felt good to be out of there. We were free from the sights and the sounds of the party, and the fresh air felt so good. The breeze that brushed upon our little faces, blew all the pain away from our unconscious minds.

I felt like shouting at our father. How badly I wanted to tell him how we were really feeling. How disappointed Jim and I were. How we once again had trusted him to make sure we were safe and happy. We didn't shout at him because, well, because he was our dad and we wanted him to love us. "Honor thy father and thy mother," was one of the Ten Commandments, after all.

The next morning finally did come. Jim woke up first, then, he woke me up. There wasn't anyone stirring in the apartment yet, so we just waited to see what would happen. You talk about living on the edge, well, when you grow up with alcoholics, you are always on the edge. It's like constantly being on the edge of a cliff, hundreds of feet high, feeling like just before your feet leave that solid place, you just don't know where you'll land, or if you'll be alright!

Soon after, Uncle Henry rose to greet us. He made us breakfast and told us that we would be taking a tour of Montreal, Canada. He explained that our dad wasn't up for the trip and would not be coming with us. It would be just my brother Jim and me.

Jim was around twelve mind you, and I was fourteen, and here we were boarding a bus that would take us around a huge city, with strangers. A bus full of STRANGERS! Not one adult we knew to accompany us on our bus ride. We toured the city alone. I had to become the adult, once again, and looked out for my younger brother. And to think, I didn't even raise my hand for the job.

Dressed in our Sunday best we traveled through the streets of Montreal. The tour was not geared to the interests of children, but adults, with stops at attractions like exquisite flower gardens and lavish churches, but we made the best of it. It was much better than watching adults getting drunk.

As we drove back into the bus station where the tour had departed from earlier, I eagerly looked out the window hoping to catch a glimpse of my father waiting for us. There, waiting in front of the building was none other than Uncle Henry, with my dad nowhere in sight. Henry explained that my dad wasn't feeling well, that he was resting, and he would take us back to the apartment. My heart sank. Once again, he had let us down. Once again, he wasn't there for us. However, once again I would forgive him. I felt I had to; he was our father. Maybe he would be better tomorrow.

Funny thing, I always believed that the drinking would stop. That someday my dad would notice Jim and I, and be glad that we were there. That he would realize that he had a wonderful son and daughter who only wanted to BE LOVED. Not now though, not at this point in time.

He did come around, a little, years later; but for now my dears, you must take out those rose-colored glasses, and put them on, and carry on. They will help to numb all the fear and shame you are feeling, and give you the faith and outrageous hope you need to surrive.

ANOTHER DAY HAD passed, and we had been very neglected. The drinking was the priority, as we knew it would be. The difference here was that we were hundreds of miles away from home. In another country. Jim and I had no place to run to, no place to hide, and now fear began to set in. Uncle Henry was understanding, but a lot like the other warm bodies around. "Oh I wish I could get your dad to stop drinking," he had said. However, words without action are simply that, just WORDS.

It was time once again to dig deep down inside as I told myself, "You are on your own on this one kiddo," and then and there I decided to call my grandparents. I was hoping that the sound of my grandfather's voice, in particular, could sober him up very quickly. Kind of like the voice of GOD, because that is the kind of fear my grandfather could, and did, evoke in you.

So, I asked to use the phone. My Uncle Henry was very accommodating, and helped with the procedure for calling out of the country. I remember being so anxious. Will they answer? Are they home?

"Oh, please answer. Please, please, PLEASE pick up the receiver," I said with my inside screaming voice! I stood there in the kitchen, frozen in time, and waited for someone to answer the telephone. Finally, after what seemed like an eternity, my grandfather did pick up the receiver! I tried to keep it together, but I couldn't, and through desperate, quiet sobs, tears rolling down my cheeks, I begged my grandfather to talk to Dad, and to tell him to take us home.

I called to Dad who was in the living room. I said that my grandfather wanted to talk to him. Luckily, since I was in the kitchen, I had time to pull myself together as best I could before Dad came close enough to get the phone. There was a lot of listening going on from Dad's end on the phone, as I watched my father shake his head several times and respond with, "Yes Jim, okay Jim, you're right Jim." Something to that effect.

Whatever my grandfather said worked like a charm, because the very next day we were on our way back to the USA, to New England, to New Hampshire. Home sweet home!

༄

IT SEEMED LIKE we would never arrive at our destination, HOME. However, the ride was through Franconia Notch, and the mountains surrounded us like soldiers, and somehow, I felt safe. We sat very still during our ride in the car. Dad was quiet, so we needed to be quieter, in order to please him. So Dad wouldn't get mad at us. It's called "Walking on Eggshells," and we knew that song and dance well, because it was all done "In the name of love." You've got to keep them happy, so that they'll love you, you know. Oh yes, throw in the "Honor your father and your mother" commandment, and that's it. A sealed deal. Because God is watching you, too!

And the Thunder Moon waned.

THIRTEEN

I graduated from high school. I had made plans, on my own, to further my education. A local college, Notre Dame College, in Manchester, NH, would be my choice. Then it would be possible to attend college full-time, and keep my position at Jordan Marsh, in Bedford. The money I earned would be put toward college tuition and other expenses.

I have to say that my grandfather, although dysfunctional in many ways, did believe in education, and was instrumental in my continuing on with school. He felt that education was a means of financial independence, and survival. A progressive thinker indeed, in the education department anyway, for it was the 1970s.

So, off I went to college. My physical health wasn't very good. Anorexia had turned into bulimia, and went back and forth.

For some reason my soul never, never, never gave up. There was a relentless inner strength! Call it faith, whatever, that would not allow me to give up! Going to Notre Dame College, in Manchester, NH was such a wonderful experience. It exposed me to another kind of world. A world full of so many possibilities, with still so much to do, so much to see. It brought me closer to home, to me, Kathleen.

THE TIME MACHINE has brought me back to today: Monday, July 21, 2003. My day began with a wonderful mountain run on South Uncanoonuc Mountain. I returned today by myself, an incredible feeling to know that I am still standing, still running actually, and to go back to the place where so much time was spent with someone I totally trusted, loved—at my expense, but in the name of love. Self-sacrifice and love knew no difference!

In the Name of Love

COLLEGE REALLY HELPED me to rid myself of some of the baggage that I had been carrying around. The classes were so interesting, so challenging. They gave me a new focus, which for me, at the time, was to become an elementary school teacher. I loved children, and I wanted to reach out, through education, to tell all children of the world that they had value.

While on my glorious mission, I met many other individuals with similar philosophies. So incredible, imagine that! It was one of those pivotal moments in time. I belonged; I wasn't alone anymore. What a refreshing place, with stimulating conversations, about people and places. Most of us so idealistic, hoping that we could somehow make a difference.

It was in my freshman year of college that I met Karen (Cushing) Lesko. We were so similar in nature. She was an education major like me, and we met in one of the required classes. Karen was like an angel sent down from heaven and continues to be one of my SOUL sisters. I know, lame, but oh so true! She always made me feel so comfortable, and so I began to open up and share some very personal things, like how at 18 years of age I had never had a date.

Well, she immediately dismissed it and said, "That's all right."

Karen let me, be me. Now that is indeed true friendship. She introduced me to her family, and instantly I was welcomed with open arms. Another Ah-Ha moment, with people who were so kind and generous, I truly felt like I was dreaming. And to make things even more unbelievable, she had a very cute brother, Lenny.

Karen was an instrument of my growth, better yet, someone who helped me reclaim myself. She helped me to gain confidence, find hope and gave me lots of joy and laughter.

Every time I went to Karen's home, I felt like I was home. I've never told her this, but I wanted her parents to adopt me. Not a bad deal—I did dishes and could cook!

I recall being so touched when Karen and her mother surprised me with gifts for my birthday. To show that they cared about me was one of the nicest things that anyone had ever done! Karen had bought me a little statue that represented the month I was born in, and her mother presented me with a four-inch statue of a leprechaun, paying tribute to my Irish ancestry. Just to have someone take the time to remember you on your birthday was a kind gesture I would always treasure. Why, I still have the August statue with me, right here in my current residence, and the value lies not in the piece, but the love with which it was given, making it truly "priceless."

I have since given the leprechaun away. I don't remember to whom, but it was given with the hope that "Good Luck" would bless that person forever! The luck of the Irish was something I always held dear to my heart. If nothing else could protect me, surely the luck part would kick in, and I would be saved.

YOU'VE HEARD THE expression "breaking out of your shell." Well, Karen certainly helped me in that department, too. For whenever her family would have a party, they would always include me. I mean all sorts of events. Everything from birthday parties to wedding anniversaries.

The parties in her basement were the most fun of all! We would congregate there. First, there was lots of silence. Len, Karen's brother who was a year younger than Karen, and who I had a serious crush on, would be there, along with lots of his other single available friends. The pickings were good, and the bonus was that they all liked to DANCE!

I never really got to hit it off with her brother, and as I look back now, I realize I was much too thin. I was still struggling with anorexia. The illness had also affected my teeth something fierce. It came to the point that when I would eat something hard I would have a tooth that would simply fall apart. Crumble, as I was still crumbling inside.

Shhh...Be silent. We must protect our elders. Honor them?

So, in the name of God's love, I did.

My father wouldn't pay for caps for some of my teeth, they were just too expensive, you see. So, the dentist we had at the time would just pull the teeth out, instead of trying to save them. Sometimes, just sometimes, I wished he'd pull out all the pain inside too! Couldn't he see what was going on? Couldn't he?

As I returned again and again, not once did he ever inquire about what might be happening to me. Not once! He knew that I was just a child, too. About fifteen or so at the time, and that I had no means of being able to make payment for any services rendered. I learned later that the teeth could have been saved, too!

I even recall, one time when I had two teeth pulled, I lost some blood and was a little too weak—from the extractions and the Novocain—to walk home, which was about four miles away. Anyway, I needed a ride, and the receptionist at the dentist's office had tried to reach my dad, without any luck. So, they went ahead and called a taxi for me to make sure I would make it home all right. Off I rode in the back seat of the taxi cab, and I did make it home safe, but not sound. For when my dad arrived home he went into hysterics over the cost of the taxi. He then proceeded to call the dentist's office, and told them, "Don't you ever call a taxi for her again, she can walk home no matter what condition she is in!"

Well, I got the message loud and clear. I had cost him money, and had bothered him with a problem! This was NEVER to happen again. So, it never did, and in the name of God's love, I forgave him, because my dad didn't love me, and I wanted him to so, so badly.

So, by the age of 18 I was quite a sight. I couldn't laugh about it, just cry alone in the living room when nobody was home. The tears helped to wash away all the sadness, and I prayed for the strength and the courage to carry on.

Along with paying for college, clothes and the gas for my car, I saved to have my teeth fixed. I wanted to be able to smile again, because when you have nice pearly whites, you can smile, and then laugh, and smiling and laughing can smooth out the rough edges in this life. They help to comfort the soul.

In the Name of Love

THINKING BACK TO that time, 1975, that place, I remember Karen and her family like it was yesterday. So clear, so vivid, with the gentle warmth of smiles and words each time I entered their home. It elicited a wonderful feeling of being of value. To slowly get Kathleen back, or at least catch a small glimpse of someone lost a long time ago.

In a short time I had become very close to Karen's whole family, and in a way it felt like the family that I never had. Karen's mother, in particular, would take the time to listen to me, and talk to me too. Wow, it felt so incredible! I hope I remembered to say thank you to her.

When you become close to people, with friends and some acquaintances, you get to know all about their lives. I remember one day, shortly after she had become engaged to be married, Karen told me something about her mom. She told me that her mother was suffering from cancer. Her strength was diminishing daily, and Karen was even troubled now by the thought that her mom would not be able to make her wedding.

In the midst of this sorrow, the festivities were still planned. I was asked to be in the wedding party. I was to be a bridesmaid. I wasn't sure about saying yes to her, I was so afraid of stepping out of my world. But somehow, Karen made me feel confident, like it would be such fun, and it was!

I just loved the whole idea of being a bridesmaid, and when I finally was able take the dress home, I must have tried it on a million times!

I remember feeling like a princess. Like I was Cinderella, and maybe, just maybe, there would be a prince for this young maiden, who didn't want to be an old maid! I smiled back at the mirror. I knew I was ready!

IT WAS KAREN and her family who brought me to this path, this new road, and as I went to her home that October morning in 1975 to prepare to be in her wedding, something happened. Kathleen emerged, and a small part would forever live on! With much more to be unveiled at a much later date.

Karen looked like an angel, so elegant and lady like, and yet the essence of her innocence surrounded her. It was a bittersweet moment, as I recall, feeling happy and sad at the same time. Sad, that I had to share her, because now she was a wife, adding another hat to her head. The role of daughter, substitute mother and sister had already been claiming her time.

I was happy also, because at that time it seemed to be something that she really, really wanted. And, when you love someone, you don't try to control them, you set them free! So, I smiled on that day, and I let my friend be, as tears ran down my blushed cheeks during the exchange of their vows. She was now MRS. LESKO.

We left the church and went on to the reception hall. This was going to be so much fun, you could feel the excitement in the air! After all the formalities were completed, the dinner, the clinking of glasses to get the newlyweds to kiss, and the dollar dance, the DANCING could begin.

The lyrics from one of the songs in the movie Dirty Dancing, "Now I'm having the time of my life," certainly captured the mood of that day. I got to dance the evening away, and it wasn't so much who I danced with, but much more about the fact that someone wanted to dance with me! Someone thought I was worthy of dancing with them, of talking to them. To just be myself was all right. Another pivotal moment in time!

WHEN THE SPRING of 1976 came, it took away the snow, but it was also took away the life of Karen's mother, a beautiful women, who was loved by many.

The death of Karen's mom brought to my conscious mind the question of this life. The whys mostly, and the hardest part is that with some things you experience, it seems like you'll never find the answer. It is there though, if you keep believing.

In the fall, Karen did not return to school. As I understood it, her father Bob, had told her to stay home and care for her two younger brothers, a surrogate mother of sorts. Someone had to care for the family now.

I was so upset with the situation. Karen was so smart, so creative, brave and true! I couldn't help but wonder what *she* wanted. To me it was such an injustice! Here was a young woman with such a great gift to give to the world and, in my opinion, her future was stolen from her. Vultures and thieves were all around I thought, and I was simply infuriated at this new order!

However, in the name of love, Karen did what she thought she should do, not what she wanted. She took a path that would lead her to many places she thought she would never go to. Her story is one of strength and courage, a superhero who refuses to wear a red cape.

So, I went on to my third year of college with a new perspective on this world. I had lost two dear people that year. Jean, Karen's mom was one, due to death. Karen was the other, due to life. Oh, Karen and I were still friends, but it would be different now. For she had become a wife, a surrogate mother, and soon she would be a mother herself. Limited amount of time left over to just chill with a friend. The changes were so hard, but we did not resist them, we embraced them. And our friendship, well, it did withstand the tests of time, and to this day, it is something that I cherish.

True friends are just like an echo, you get back what you give, sometimes even more, but you never leave with less.

And the Thunder Moon waxed.

FOURTEEN

LIFE IS CERTAINLY a journey, and Karen had prepared me for the next chapter of my life. At Karen's wedding I had met John. A guy who was nice to look at, smart and had a very good nature. I was able to fill my dance card on that day of celebration, and oh life felt SIMPLY DELICIOUS! We exchanged numbers, and we were to go out on a date the following weekend, as I recall.

The following evening I had plans to go out dancing at a local bar with live, great music. There on that night, I met yet another very dashing, (and as I had written in my journal, "Debonair") guy, Chuck.

Chuck asked me for my phone number also—must have been the perfume I was wearing. Due to the fact that we had met in a BAR, I was not just going to give it out. Pride overruled, and I told him that I might be back next week.

Talk about being on a roll. The world seemed to be at my fingertips! I was feeling mighty fine, and getting attention, which I was starving for, finally feeling like I had value. However, I was looking for value in the wrong place, as I realize now. In the back of my mind, you see, was also the haunting thought that I might be alone forever. Wow, alone, funny what you do when you don't know any better.

So, I went from not bothering at all with boys to being bothered by not only one, but two young pursuers. Life was so sweet, and it was really one of those incredible moments in time. I was seeing John *and* Chuck, and enjoying all their attention and company. I was not ready to be exclusive.

John was quite the gentlemen. He would open doors for me, and never used vulgar language, definitely a positive character trait from a Catholic girl's point of view. He was so thoughtful too, surprising me with a phone call to join him for lunch every now and then. John was very handsome, and my grandmother approved of him. I think it was because he was Polish, and one of her very best friends when she was growing up was Polish (therefore, making all attractive Polish men a good catch, through some strange logic).

Chuck, on the other hand was very adventurous. When I met him he was a scuba diver. He loved the outdoors, and did things like tennis, hiking, cross-country skiing, and he loved to dance. He was not the kind of person to sit around a lot, and I think that was the reason why I liked him a little more. You see, I wanted to be moving and grooving, and most of our weekends were spent doing something exciting together. It was a whole new fabulous world for me.

JOHN AND I were going to double date with another couple, Michelle and Jim. Michelle and I knew one another from when we both attended Notre Dame College. We were in some classes together and had become friends. I met Jim a couple of times when he had picked up Michelle. So, I thought we'd all have a good time together.

Well, we had decided to meet at the movie theatre. As I was introducing John to Michelle and Jim, I accidentally said, "This is Chuck."

As the words were rolling off my tongue, I couldn't believe that I said them! I was simply stupefied by my slip, and the look on John's face told me that there was no place to run to, no place to hide. He had heard me loud and clear. As I struggled for some lame explanation, I could feel a cold sweat cover my entire body. John's reply was quite justified as he responded with, "Chuck, who's Chuck?" in a very loud whisper.

I was so grateful that we were in a movie theatre, because loud voices were frowned upon. I laughed a nervous laugh, and quickly shrugged it off as just someone I knew, which was true, or something—I don't recall verbatim what my response was.

The movie began within minutes of this awkward introduction, which gave me time to think of a way to explain, and to regain my composure. Thank goodness, for in those days, the seventies, there weren't many previews.

As they say, the jig was up, and I did have some explaining to do. I had been dating two guys for about four months, but it was not on this night that I was ready to share that information. The truth was soon to come out. Funny how the truth sets you free, even when you might not want to be set free.

IT WAS ON another evening when I was going to the local college, SNHU, to hear a live band called Broan and Hogman, that the drama would unfold. Here we were, John and I. I can even remember vividly where we were sitting, and that I was wearing. My favorite sage green corduroys, a yellow short-sleeve knit top that hugged my upper body nicely, and a scarf twisted around my neck tied into a small bow in the front. Hey, it was the seventies.

John had started celebrating before picking me up, so when we arrived at the show, he was, shall we say, feeling no pain! Frankly, this really annoyed me! It brought back memories of the past, times when family members were intoxicated and obnoxious, as he was becoming. It is extremely embarrassing for the innocent non-drinkers because they can see and hear everything, unlike the drinkers.

Well, the music that the band was playing was excellent. Great tunes to dance to, and I love to dance! So, I forgave the condition that John was in, and we danced until the band took their break.

Break time is just that, and with all the ginger ale I had consumed it was time for a trip to the ladies room. On the way there, low and behold, who do I run into but, CHUCK!

I could hardly believe my eyes.

He asked me who I was there with, and without further complicating things, I simply told him.

"Oh, I'm here with John." I mean it rolled off my tongue, just like that. I thought it better to act just like everything was the way it should be. On that night a decision needed to be made, John or Chuck. The double dating was over! John was clear about wanting to be exclusive, and so was Chuck. There was no question, Chuck won for me at the time, hands down.

In the Name of Love

TODAY IS OCTOBER 9, 2003. I began this day with great thoughts of going to run the Applefest Half Marathon, in glorious Hollis, NH. On the way to meet my friends that I would be going with, I had a frightening sighting! Someone who tortured me for no reason, a real live predator!

The sighting took place around 7am as I was heading north on Mammoth Road. The predator, as I will refer to him—my head won't allow my hands to write his name, nor speak of it, ever again, in honor of me—was parked on the left side of the street. He was next to the park there, just waiting.

I saw the truck parked about a quarter of a mile or so before I reached it, not quite sure it was his vehicle, trying to remain calm and cautious, and not paranoid. As I adjusted my eyes, to make sure that this was not just an illusion, reality hit me—it was in fact HIM, the predator!

I was frozen at first. "Oh my God," I said to myself, trying to stay in control of my Chevy pick-up truck and telling myself that it was just a coincidence. That's it, just a coincidence! Even after almost three years, that terrifying feeing was still present. It doesn't pack the same power that it used to, the fight or flight response, because now I am in the driver's seat. Now, I can calm myself by thinking of things that are joyful and peaceful. Things like my two beautiful daughters, friends, and trail running in my favorite places. Zapping those horrible, nightmarish memories like a backyard bug zapper.

I continued on down Mammoth Road and turned left onto Bridge Street. My gut just kept tugging at me that he was following me, and as I passed an officer doing roadside duty, I was very tempted to pull over and ask for his protection. However, with all I've been through, and the lack of support from the police, my lawyer, and the probation department, I no longer have faith in authority figures. I decided against it.

Sure enough, gut feelings are the essence of your soul, talking to you, so always pay close attention, because as I came to the intersection of Elm Street and Bridge, there he was, right behind me! I quickly pulled into the far left-hand lane, hoping that he wouldn't have enough time to pull into that lane, because that was the direction I was headed. I didn't even use my directional so he wouldn't follow.

Luckily, two or three cars pulled up behind me to make the same turn. He then went by me heading west, straight across Elm Street, to continue going over the Bridge Street bridge.

I seemed to have lost him, and it was comforting to know that I would soon be meeting my two friends, one of whom was a six foot male, and he was running in the Clydesdale division. Thank you, God!

It was quite ironic that the song on the radio station I was listening to, 93.7, at the moment his truck passed by was "Fighter" by Christina Aguilera. The words were so, so profound, and they rang true, loud and clear!

DAYS PASSED, AS did the weeks and the months. I dated Chuck for about a year and a half, and in May of 1977, he proposed to me. When I look back now, the proposal was so pitiful. So unlike anything I would have ever wanted. He simply pulled over to the side of the road and said something like, "Here, do you want to be my wife?"

Karen had been married in October of 1975, and it had seemed like a fairy tale come to true to be married. So, in the name of love of "Fairy Tales," I decided that this would be my next adventure.

The wedding date was set for November 24, 1977, Thanksgiving Day. Anyway, it would be a morning ceremony, the time and date set to accommodate his family business. Now is that a red flag or what? And after all, we must please others, not ourselves. So, in the name of love, and wanting his family to accept me, I was a doormat once again. At least we served turkey, stuffing, gravy and cranberry sauce at the reception!

I did not have a clue as to what I was agreeing to when I exchanged vows on that day. I really feel that in most cases, people don't really share any of the horrors of marriage. Unless you are on the same page, without either one thinking that you will change the other, it is a disaster from the get go. Love, in my opinion, does nothing to change the core of a person, because as the song goes by Patty Smyth and Don Henley, "Sometimes love just ain't enough!"

Values are the essence of who you are, what you are, your soul, I believe. Lots of women don't even know who they are when they are young, and they often times make the discovery long after. I know I did.

Time, children, dinners out, sexy underwear, orgasms, flowers, hiking, and biking are all distractions. They never, ever make up for another human being with whom you can connect. It has to be soul to soul to last.

Not to judge here about who is good and not so good. It's just that if you don't like green olives, no matter what you do, you'll never like them! Olives aren't bad. They're just something that you don't want.

THE GREATEST PART of our union, Chuck's and mine, was our children. The first miracle arrived on February 14, 1980, a precious Valentine package, a daughter, Kristen Ann, our sweetheart.

I could barely keep my composure, as I came to the realization that this gift was ours. I had been told many years ago, due to an illness, that there was a possibility that I wouldn't be able to conceive, and since I had had a miscarriage with my first child after three months, having Kristen was an unexpected gift, almost incomprehensible!

This was truly another adventure for me, and I was so happy that I could finally be a mother. It was extremely important to me to be the best I could be, and in many ways I wanted to give my children what I never had.

Two years later, on February 17, 1982, Sarah Elizabeth arrived. A blessing from above that had come into our lives. Another daughter, our "Sunshine," nicknamed by her Grampy Rioux, because she was such a happy child.

Motherhood was an important job to me. One which I took very seriously. I figured that I had brought these children into the world, and therefore it was my responsibility to care for them, full-time. I just could not bring myself to put them into a daycare setting. I had tried to put Kristen in a daycare for about two months, but I was heartbroken every single time I dropped her off. Kristen was my precious package, and it seemed to me like I was giving her away to be raised by someone else. I just couldn't bear it. So, against my husband's wishes, I broke a teaching contract to be a stay-at-home mom. Indeed, this was one of those pivotal moments, when some things that are said and done can never be taken back.

Different beliefs and different values are your core. They can never, ever be changed. It's not about right or wrong, it's just about what the TWO of you, as a married couple, want. You can even discuss beforehand topics such as child rearing and be in agreement, but when it really happens, well, that's a whole different thing.

KRISTEN ANN WAS a delightful child. Being the first, I feel for her, a lot of trial and error for the first-born for sure! You want the first born to be so perfect, and never having been a parent, all the things that your child does seem to be a direct reflection on your parenting skills.

Kristen was always so compliant, so creative and willing to try almost anything. She had dabbled in ballet, Brownies, art lessons, and soccer all by the time she was eight. She never complained about anything, and as she did all her activities, I was fortunate enough to learn along with her about so many things. I was also able to meet some very interesting parents, teachers and coaches. So, to you Kristen, my lucky charm, I say THANK YOU!

Kristen was an amazing reader too. She was able to read by the time she was about four, and from that point on, there was no stopping her! I tried to read to her every night.

As she grew, I sometimes found it difficult to let her spread her wings. It was my problem though, not hers. I wasn't very flexible at times. I wasn't always a lawyer acting in her defense, but sometimes became the judge, which only builds walls, not bridges. But, I didn't know better then.

Kristen is Kristen, just as it should be. I love her all ways, always!

She is kind, patient, creative and a beautiful young woman now, and I am so very lucky to have a daughter like her.

She is not me, Kathleen, thank goodness! One is enough in the world!

SARAH ELIZABETH WAS our second child. A gift bestowed upon us on February 17, 1982, another daughter, and as much as Kristen was compliant, Sarah was not. Understand, however, that I say that in a most loving way, because now I understand.

While you are raising an extremely strong-willed child, along with all the other daily responsibilities, you truly fail to appreciate that fine quality of a child who is an independent thinker! Sarah was her own person, bless her, and the trouble was that I thought I knew more than she. What was I thinking?

For, most of the time, she made perfect sense.

Yes, Sarah Elizabeth did her own thing. She refused to play organized sports, or do any activity where there was some adult telling children what to do. She had tried soccer for about a week, and quit. She informed her father and I that, "If I want to learn how to play soccer, I can buy a book and teach myself."

It seemed to me that often times she had the answers even before you asked the questions! Which can be a little intimidating when you're an adult, because typically, you should know more than your six-year old child does.

Sarah is quick witted, and she can always see humor in many situations. It is an especially useful skill when life keeps shooting arrows at you—the humor becomes your shield. Made to take on even the most life-threatening challenges, which I can personally attest to.

Like when I was incarcerated, in jail, and I made my first phone call to Sarah. Needing and wanting to hear a voice of hope. First, I apologized to her for causing her any pain or embarrassment. Then, I made some remark as to the present situation, and the mess I had gotten myself into.

There was silence on the other end of the telephone and then,

"Mom, there is only one way to go, and that's up." Well, I was so overcome with different emotions that I was laughing and crying at the same time. And at that very moment, it was those words that saved me. My daughter loved me unconditionally. Something I had done for others, but had never been done for me. Sarah had made me realize that this was not the end, but the beginning of another chapter in my life.

I replied back, trying to use humor to heal, that, "It was a good thing I changed my last name. Maybe nobody will make the connection that I'm your mother."

We both shared a laugh at that. I then used my hands to dry the tears from my cheeks.

Kristen and Sarah are the lights in my life! Raising the girls had brought me to people and places I would have never dared to venture to. For to me, children give us so much if we take time to be with them, and to listen to them too. To receive their gifts.

Motherhood has made me a very, very, very rich women.

And the Thunder Moon waxed.

FIFTEEN

MY MARRIAGE WAS a journey. I was married on November 24, 1977, until I filed for a divorce in June of 1998. When I had made my decision to marry, no one could have talked me out of it. It was something I had to go through in order to get to where I am today. "You *allow* people to treat you the way they do." Someone once said that to me after I filed for divorce, and those words were like a punch into reality! Too bad I did not take heed to their truth at that time.

I am grateful that I was married and had the opportunity to be a wife. What I hold onto are the wonderful moments in time, the times that were filled with joy and laughter. I learned many things from my marriage to Chuck, things that I would have never known, and for that experience I say, "Thank you," to him. Now I am Stronger, Wiser, and a Fighter!

The relationship was something I did not want anymore, and in the name of loving Kathleen, I left.

However, the reaction of my children, family and some friends took my breath away, and instead of honoring what was best for me, they threw words at me. Sticks and stones might have been better, at least they don't stick to your mind.

Now, I don't care what anyone thinks of me! Back then, I thought that if I made a decision, like divorce, and that I was happy, my friends and family would be supportive, understanding, and by my side.

HA! What was I thinking?

The comments and the questions were beyond belief. People would say things like, "He doesn't seem that bad." Or, as one of my older family members blurted out, "He was always nice to me, I like him."

I was finally being honest about my life and what I wanted from it, but they didn't believe me! They were suspicious, and just about called me a liar, and it hurt like hell at the time!

What it comes done to is the real truth. They didn't live with him, I did! The trouble was that I did such a fine job of covering up for him, and putting on a happy face, that they didn't want to believe it, they almost couldn't. My performance was of Oscar quality!

I finally had the courage to take a stand and file for a divorce, after years of being where I did not want to be. I had met another man, and for once in my life I put myself first. That I had become involved with another man before the divorce was finalized complicated things, but it also brought the realization that my marriage had been over for a while.

I MET THE PREDATOR in the early 90's. It was at the end of summer, I believe. My husband and I were outside in our driveway talking to our neighbors, when out of nowhere, a car we were unfamiliar with pulled up alongside the curb that was in front of our house. The car stopped, parked and then a man I had never seen before stepped out.

As the predator walked towards us, I noticed that he looked like a man who was filled with confidence, bordering on arrogance, he was like a cool breeze on a hot summer day; you noticed. He had a big smile on his face, appeared to be healthy and in good physical shape.

He approached my husband first, holding his hand out for Chuck to shake while introducing himself. Then, he came over to where I was standing and said hello. I in turn, shook his outstretched hand and said, "Hi, I'm Kathy." I remember thinking, *I felt something.*

He said that he had shopped at the store my husband owned. Chuck seemed even friendlier after he shared that he was a customer, like a politician, pretending that he remembered him or something. The man went on to say how he had seen us running, and that he was a runner himself, but he preferred running the trails on the Uncanoonuc Mountains in Goffstown.

"Have you ever run on them?" he asked.

In unison we replied that we hadn't run on the trails, but we had hiked them. Well, that seemed to be the cue to open the floodgate of his trail running adventures.

He was animated as he spoke about his trail running adventures and the races he had run. He was flirtatious and made eye contact with me as he rambled on and on. I was captivated, to say the least! Someone was showing me some attention.

I had not shown up for my own life very much lately. And somehow, the predator had unleashed the fearless and adventurous giant that had lain dormant for so many years. He had dug his talons of freedom into my psyche, and I wanted to go run the trails at that moment.

Due to the alienation, at the time, of my family and friends, he appeared to be the only one who I thought believed in me.

Just writing that last line now seems so pitiful. LUST and LOVE begin with the same letter, but end up in disaster when the two people aren't living the same truth. I was pulled into a fantasy world once again!

AROUND SEPTEMBER OF 1998 I moved out of the home I had been residing in for years. After the courts had awarded me alimony, I ventured out into the world. I left behind my sixteen year old, who had decided to live with her father and not me. I did not want to have her uprooted, so I thought, foolishly, it better if I moved out.

My eighteen year old, Kristen Ann, had just started college. I am so sorry, now, that Kristen's memories of her moment of glory—graduating from high school and going off to college—are tainted with memories of her father and I getting a divorce. But I didn't know any better. I really was doing the best I knew how to then.

MY DAD HAD lived within a mile of my home on Mason Street, and he didn't want me to be very far away from him. So, he found this quaint little one bedroom, with a small den, a tiny kitchen and a porch, all on the second floor. Of course, this added one more pressure to my life, Dad's needs.

Instead of thinking of what *I* wanted, I returned to focusing on everyone else, and in the name of love, I did all the things that I felt I should do.

THR FIRST HOLIDAY after I moved out was Thanksgiving. I recall how painful it was when my daughters didn't come for dinner, but instead chose to dine with their father. He had prepared a meal, his first mind you, and we were all invited to come.

I refused to go, so I was left all alone. There wasn't even a phone call to let me know about their decision. They never even came for dessert! What had I done? Now they, too, didn't love me anymore. I felt like I had lost my children because of a choice I had made, and it all seemed so unfair at the time. Horrible! I couldn't believe it!

So, on that particular Thanksgiving Day, I wasn't feeling so thankful. Instead, I cried, I mean right in front of my dad. It all just came pouring out. I wasn't able to compose myself any longer, especially after hours of waiting and hoping that they would show up.

I felt so betrayed at the time, but now I understand: they were hurting too. I had hurt them. They were doing the best that they could. In the name of love, I took the blame that day, instead of working on what I needed to do to get myself together. I didn't share my real feelings of being hurt by the actions of my daughters. I just bore the cross, and suffered it.

THERE WERE SO many adjustments to being "Out There." I mean out there in the sense of supporting myself financially. The working world was a whole new world for me. There were few people who seemed to care, but the purpose of work was to work. For when you are a stay-at-home mom primarily, you are your own boss, working on your own time, at your own pace. You get everything done, but when you want.

I had worked outside the home, mostly evenings and weekends mind you, so I was not completely sheltered from the world, but part-time is very different from a full-time situation.

So, I was not only dealing with my personal life, I was dealing with the world of work, and all that it was NOT!

The man I had become involved with was married, which was just adding more drama to my life. The running, biking and numerous sexual encounters with him were like morphine, barely keeping me alive. The red flags of this abusive relationship went unrecognized as the drug of the relationship had taken over. I deserved whatever I got because I filed for divorce and got involved with a married man. He even accused me of breaking up his marriage!

I believed I wasn't worthy of anything good, and this psychological situation made me easy prey for this man, who turned out to be a PREDATOR, more dangerous than I could have imagined.

IN JANURY OF 2000 all hell began to break loose. Guilt, shame and fear were chasing me, and I couldn't run fast enough!

I went downstairs to pick up my mail. My mailbox was located on the landing of the first-floor porch. As I was going through my mail, just as I had on any other day since I had moved out of my Mason Street home, I came across an envelope that was different.

The envelope was small, the size that would hold a Thank You note, an invitation to a birthday party or maybe a wedding shower of some sort. I was very curious to open it, as I noticed that my name had been type-written, with no return address on it. I opened the envelope and pulled out a notecard with a floral bouquet on the front, with no message on it. My curiosity was peaked now, and I opened up the card and found the message inside typewritten as well.

As I read the typed message I began to shake and tremble. I freaked out as I comprehended the words I read: *You adulteress, You sinner! How would you like your daughters to know what you have been doing? REPENT! SINNER! BAD KARMA TO YOU!*

Adulteress was an uncomfortable word, so was sinner, but the idea that someone was going to tell my daughters about my actions put a sword right through my heart.

I was devastated, and this was the beginning of the end of the old

Kathleen. I just couldn't believe that someone knew about our affair, and I can't even say love affair, because it wasn't! That someone was watching us, and evil enough to use this to gain control. The hands of guilt, fear and shame were around my neck, and they were slowly strangling me. A darkness I had never, ever known before had punctured my soul, and it was soaking in, little by little, drowning the hope.

I vividly remember that I was in the den of my apartment and that it was early afternoon when I opened the first letter. It was just like when you heard about the assassination of President Kennedy, a frozen moment in time, where you can recall everything exactly, all the sights, the sounds and the smells.

Questions whirled in my mind like a tornado. Who was this letter from? Why were they sending it to me? Who was the coward who had typed it and then mailed it to me? Why not confront me? I felt so helpless at not having any of the answers!

MY FIRST GUESS was my soon to be ex-husband. He was looking to settle our divorce. Or, maybe it was the predator's wife, or one of his daughters. It was like something out of a horror movie, really, like, "I know what you've been doing with him."

You see, at the time, I hadn't told my daughters about my involvement with the predator. I felt that if they knew that, they would never speak to me again. They would think the reason I left their father was because of another man, when in reality, IT WAS NOT!

What little confidence that I had gained in myself was wiped out at that moment! The current of life had thrown me into the riptide, and I was drowning with guilt, fear and shame.

Whoever sent that first letter knew exactly what they were doing. The coward! For even to this day, I don't know who sent it. The predator said that one was sent to him, too. I have a hard time believing this, due to the source of course.

In February of 2000 another letter arrived. Just like the one before it, the address on the front of the envelope was type written, the contents of the message typed as well. It was like a *Halloween* movie sequel,

I did not know who was behind the letter, just like the mask of Jason. This was one letter too many, now I needed to take action, or so I thought. The Jasons of the world were really out there, nightmares were coming true.

Intimidation is all about fear. It's too bad that I did not stand my ground, but there were just too many things pulling me down. So, in the name of the love of my daughters, and my family, I decided I needed to move, to run, to take flight! Kristen and Sarah were so important to me. They were the loves of my life.

Whoever did this despicable thing knew what my Achilles' heel was, and the information of my involvement with another man was the arrow sent flying with the intention of death, the death of my relationship with my children. To think that my daughters might never speak to me again was like death to me, at least that was what I believed then. Flight mode kicked in now. Run, my dear Kathleen, RUN!

SO, I CALLED an uncle and an aunt and explained my situation. The grave concern I had for my safety, and about the letters that I had received. They had a few spare bedrooms because their children were grown and gone, and I asked if I could move in with them.

Their answer only validated my growing shame. It was no, I could not live with them! Just like that. It was another blow. I mean I had some faith in my family, up until then at least. I had always been there for any of them whenever I could be, or would have guided anyone of my family members toward where they might find help. I had expected them to help me, and I was wrong. I felt so overwhelmed. I began to crumble a little more. The words and actions of those around me were only pointing more and more to that buried voice inside of me that was now becoming louder.

"You don't have any value."

I was becoming a victim, a role I had never played before, despite everything that had happened in my childhood. I had always kept my spirit. So, in a panic, I wrote a letter to the predator. I told him that this relationship was not working. I asked him if he was ever going to leave his wife like he had said he would. His response a few days later when I met him was "No, never." And now with this new information, that was it for me.

It had taken so much strength to write the letter, and I had convinced myself because of the things that he had said and done at the time, that he was THE ONE!

Yes, he was the one all right. The one that would bring me to a place that I had never, ever been before.

I began to frantically look for another place to live. That's it, just run away, far away. So I would not see him, hear his voice or see his black truck drive by, or park in the street by my apartment. The trouble was, at this point in time, he had become intertwined into my daily life. It had happened slowly, and there was no denying that I thought he was the air that I needed to live on. A drug I had become addicted to. I was so blinded by the emotional blackmail that I couldn't leave, I couldn't see.

The relationship between the predator and I was a one-way street, where I did pretty much whatever he wanted, just because I wanted his love. When you don't love yourself, you just want someone to love you. You need them, but you really don't want them!

I wouldn't tell anyone where I was going, for fear he would find me. I also thought that now there would be serious consequences to be paid for my behavior from my children and his wife. Contoocook, NH would be the place that I would now call home. It was far enough away from Manchester, NH, and yet would be close enough to see Sarah, my youngest daughter who lived in Manchester with her father.

That decision, however, was the one that came back to haunt me; it was all wrong. But the cross, made of shame and guilt, which I had nailed myself to, was killing me. I couldn't see the right path.

I felt like I was standing all alone. Hopelessness and despair were consuming me.

BEFORE THE MOVE, I decided to take a trip with Sarah to Las Vegas, Nevada. It was an affordable trip, and it seemed like we were both shell-shocked, with the divorce and all. Trying to pretend that we were fine.

It was really an opportunity to escape—aren't all vacations? I thought it would be a good time to get re-acquainted with my youngest daughter. I had invited Kristen to come along also, but she was already headed to Florida with Andy, her boyfriend at the time.

I was able to get a week off from my position as an educational assistant in Goffstown. My supervisor, Mrs. Colby, was so understanding I couldn't believe it. Considering how vague my explanation was. "I just need to get away."

However, she granted me my request for the time off. I was so grateful!

I had only told a select few close friends where I was going with Sarah. People that I trusted and felt close to at the time. I didn't want them to worry about me. They were supportive, and agreed that a vacation would be good.

I still hadn't told anyone about the letters.

A WEEK OR so before heading out to Las Vegas, I had a close encounter of the traumatic kind. I had just finished working at school and I was proceeding to the place where I had parked my car. I located it (you can forget where you parked your car after a busy day at school), and got into my pick-up truck. As I was taking out my keys to put them into the ignition, I glanced over to the passenger side, because someone was trying to get in!

It was a male, and he just opened the door and hopped inside before I had any time to lock the door.

It was the predator!

He grabbed my wrist and said that he needed to talk to me. I mean where was I going, really? And I didn't have any time to respond truthfully. My pure instinct at the time was to submit, to LISTEN, as I am sure he knew I would. He said that his wife had found out about us, and that she was going to file for a divorce. He said, "I love you," and something to the effect that, "I don't want to lose you!"

Truthfully, I didn't really pay much attention to the rest of the conversation, because quite frankly after he said "I love you," I melted, my Achilles heel pierced once again. It was one of the weakest things I ever did, but I took him back. I felt guilty that his long marriage had broken up. He told me that is was because of our affair. Yes, it was my fault.

So, in the name of love of the predator, I surrendered. I even spilled my guts about where I had moved to, like he owned me.

Mistake, big mistake!

I didn't tell anyone what had happened. I was shaking inside for days; I couldn't even sleep. It was like my own body was trying to tell me to be brave and RUN!

THE LAS VEGAS trip helped Sarah and I to regroup somewhat. We did have fun. We went to the strip to see the sights. Wow, a playground for adults for sure! We dined out and shopped and took in a couple of shows. I loved being able to spend time with her. We both needed affirmation of our love for one another.

We had taken the time to talk, to listen and to laugh with each other. We even did some crying, because "crying is what gets the sad out of you." We were mourning the loss of our family of four, letting go of something that was never coming back!

While there, I must confess, I couldn't control myself. The addiction had reared its ugly head up, and the symptoms of withdrawal took over. There in Las Vegas, I needed to hear his voice.

To think I had gone to so much trouble to distance myself from the predator, and only two days into a beautiful vacation with my daughter, I still thought that I couldn't survive without him. Oh, I had it so bad!

My body was shaking as I dialed his number from the hotel lobby. I was too embarrassed to call from our hotel room, so I snuck down to the lobby, just like an addict meeting up with a dealer. When I called him at work, his boss answered, and he said that he would go to get the predator. As I waited, the anticipation was overwhelming, and I began to shiver, all over. Finally he came to the phone.

"Hello," he said, and a great sense of relief poured over me, as rejection would have put me over the edge. The fear that he might have changed his mind and that maybe in my absence he didn't love me anymore held me hostage. As he spoke, I recall having this euphoric feeling slowly take over, like I had just talked to God or something.

He talked to me! He still wanted me! The words resonated in my head over, and over, and over again. There, the junkie had had her fix.

WHEN I ARRIVED back to Manchester after our Las Vegas trek, I thought everything was going to be all right. Sarah and I had had a wonderful time. The time away had done us a world of good. However, it was just a Band-Aid on the deep gash of life, and all the problems were still there waiting for us when we came back.

Now, when I look back, I seriously could have used some counseling. Divorce is a death, and the longer you are married the more help I feel you need, but the way of my upbringing was to just STUFF it. Deal with it all! Don't complain, and I didn't. My lawyer had suggested that I get some counseling, but I felt at the time that counseling meant weakness. I told myself I wasn't weak!

Then, sometime in the spring of 2000, I helped the predator move into my Contookcook dwelling. I really didn't want him to, because now that the truth was out about our relationship, I had noticed some major changes. There was a side to the predator that I should have paid closer attention to, but I didn't.

Unfortunately, I began to forgive words and actions that I would never, ever have forgiven before. But who was I to judge, the adulteress, the sinner that I was? After all, I was so lucky to be included in the running, the biking and all those dinners out. Why, without the predator, I wouldn't be anybody, or so I was brainwashed to believe.

It was in Contookcook that a very dim light of sanity went on; his wife was kicking him out. Confusing self-sacrifice and love, and going against an unsettling feeling that I had in the depth of my very soul, I allowed him to enter my second floor home.

What a mistake!

Trouble was, I didn't have time to REALLY think about it, he asked me and I said yes. No is a word that an aspiring martyr never says at first response. It's only after you know what you are agreeing to that you come to the realization of what you should have said. Even then, you keep it to yourself, because you wouldn't want to hurt anyone, anyone but yourself of course.

His whole manner changed, and it was so reminiscent of the old days when I was growing up, that good old familiar walking on egg shells kind of feeling. Something I knew oh so very well. The fear of never knowing what was about to come: a hurricane, or a gentle breeze. Even the way he spoke to me, and the way he looked at me now, was telling me to be afraid, be very, very, afraid. However, I thought my love for him would be enough to calm any storm.

Soon his family and friends would know that he was involved with me, and having an affair, and he hated that. He had lost control! Now that the truth was ringing out loud and clear, he didn't want me at all. What he had really wanted was a side dish.

IT WAS IN the evening of our first night together. I had blocked out all the RED flags that were flying, a trick I knew very well. The rose-colored glasses were on tight, and as I lay down in my brass double bed, the night exploded into something I never, ever thought possible!

Earlier, during the day, he had moved in some of his belongings. Mostly clothing and some personal items like his bicycle, and a collection of books. He was silent, and extremely mechanical in nature, and although it was a little unnerving, I simply dismissed it as him being tired and upset over the break-up with his wife.

It was time for bed, and I prepared myself as I had other nights. The ritual of washing my face with Mary Kay cleanser, brushing my teeth, followed by sit-ups and some stretching exercises. The predator hadn't said hardly anything to me most of the day, and into the night, and by the time I was ready for bed, he was already there, under the covers, waiting for me.

As I reached over, he immediately took hold of my arm, and held it with great force. Then, he ordered me to remove my clothing because, "I want to fuck you tonight from behind."

The whole tone of his voice was so evil, it was incomprehensible. I couldn't believe what I was hearing! I sensed rage and blame in the tone of his voice, of someone crumbling fast, crumbling because he had gotten caught in a sexual relationship with someone other than his wife. I was petrified, trembling as I said, "No, I don't want to do that. I am tired tonight," hoping that some sense of decency would creep up from the depths of his soul!

He was outraged, and commanded me a second time to disrobe. He held my right arm even tighter, and I felt for sure that he was going to beat me!

"No, I don't want to," I said again, still scared of the consequences.

After I refused the second time, he threw my arm down, and abruptly pushed me off the bed. My fragile 108 lb. body slammed to the wooden floor with a loud thud. I landed on my left side so hard that I lay still for a moment to make sure I hadn't broken any limbs, and wondering what was to come next.

He then looked over the edge of the the bed and ordered: "Then sleep on the floor!" And threw down a pillow to me.

I was frozen, as pure fear washed over me, and I thanked god he had only thrown me to the floor, and not beaten the shit out of me. Then I prayed for the strength to take it. For how dare I say no to the mighty predator?

Once again, I found myself feeling like a little girl, totally helpless. And as I lay there on the cold wooden floor all night long, not sure what was going to happen to me, I didn't dare get up, or shout out, or even cry. I just kept on praying, praying to God that the morning would come quickly, and that I would still be alive.

Over, and over, and over again, I found myself trying to figure out how I had gotten myself into this mess. "Just lie still, don't get up, don't move, just try to breath quietly. Be still, be still, you are going to be all right! You are going to be all right! YOU ARE GOING TO BE

ALL RIGHT!" Those were the words I said to myself, trying to convince myself that everything was going to be fine. I was hoping that God was listening too!

FINALLY MORNING ARRIVED! It had seemed like it would never come, the darkness was inside and out that night.

He had gotten up. I could hear the shower running. Yes, today was Monday, he was getting ready for work. I didn't dare stir, still in survival mode. Just like a possum playing dead, and hoping and praying that he would just leave, that's all. My prayers were answered as I heard the door slam as he left for work. I didn't even have the strength or the courage to get up yet, but instead waited to hear the sound of the truck driving away to assure me that he was gone, and that it was safe for me to come out.

Once I felt that the coast was clear, I began to crumble. I felt like I had been in a horror film, and had escaped the clutches of the predator. Still on the floor, I began to shake uncontrollably, with sobs and tears consuming me. Sometimes no sound made its way from my mouth, as I tried desperately to comprehend last night.

In the name of love of the predator, ghosts of my childhood past began to creep in, and looking outside myself for an answer I asked God, "Why?"

I COULDN'T EVEN pull myself together enough to go to my job. My mind raced frantically for a solution to the new drama I had allowed into my life, my new home. I felt defeated once again. Out of the need to be loved and in the name of love of the predator, I had let him in.

I knew that I couldn't tell the predator that I wanted him out of my apartment, so I called my divorce lawyer at the time for some urgent advice. My attorney told me to tell him he couldn't live with me because his divorce had not been finalized, and that this living arrangement would greatly jeopardize his divorce case.

Yes, using my attorney as the scapegoat would be fine, I told myself. That way the predator's anger could be directed at someone else. Yes, I will call him at work, and then tell him he had to move out! I could avoid confrontation with him, right?

I did. I called him at work and told him the news quickly! I just let it spill out, and before he could respond, I hung up the phone. I didn't return to the apartment until I felt that he was long gone.

Once I returned, I looked all around for the fear that he might be lurking around somewhere. I had hoped that all of his belongings would be gone. In a panic, I went room to room to make sure that there would be no need for him to return for anything. I did find a few things, much to my disgust. I quickly picked them up and placed them into a plastic bag, just like they had toxic waste on them, and placed the bag into my pick-up truck. I would drop off the bag where he worked in the morning.

When morning came, I was still feeling the backlash from the hurricane of the day before. I was hoping that somehow this was all just a bad dream, and that I would wake up in another time and place. However, it was NOT, and I needed to get my act together as quickly as I could.

I got up and went to work that day, and the next day, and the day after that.

There are addictions of every type, and when you are addicted to anything the withdrawal part is excruciating! Emotional blackmail ran very deep in my veins, just like when I grew up. I had to forgive all the behavior of all the adults around me, in the hope that they would love me, value me. I was used to it, and when you don't know any better, you go back to what you know!

So, I came back to those rose-colored glasses, and put them on, and began to doubt my decision. I began to make up excuses for all his abusive behavior—dangerous business indeed. Already questioning my actions, I ran into his accountant, who was also a good friend of his, at the local grocery store. She said that his "flare up" was due to all the stress he was under. She said, "I mean who wouldn't get angry, his marriage of thirty plus years is breaking up?"

It was with those words that I immediately began to feel sorry for HIM. HE was hurting. HIS behavior, therefore, was justified. History was repeating itself, I was plummeted back in time; I was a five year old, emotionally. So, I went to where he worked, shaking uncontrollably, my body really warning me, in hindsight of course, telling me to, "Run, Kathleen, run far away from the predator."

However, I didn't listen. I wasn't going to give up on HIM. I felt like he was all I had left.

THE PREDATOR WAS confident, controlling, manipulative, and a fabulous liar. All the characteristics necessary for climbing the ladder of success, at anybody's expense, except for his.

I entered his place of employment. I was a basket case. I slowly walked towards where he was, on the east side of the room, with partitions on either side of his desk, and there he was.

As I approached him, he looked up from his paperwork. His eyes were wild looking, and I suddenly realized I really didn't know the predator very well at all. If eyes were knives, I would have been dead on the floor, as he told me in a cold, distant whisper, "Get the fuck out of here. It's over, you bitch!"

The words resonated over, over and over again, as I felt like he had ripped out my heart and left me for dead. Was this the man who I had spent so much time with, who I had eaten with, and slept with and shared my hopes and my dreams with? All in the name of love!

THIS TIME THE break-up seemed like it was true, like it was really all over. He went back to live with his wife, in the home where they had lived. She had taken him back!

I was somewhat relieved. It felt like the spell was finally broken, and that my guardian angels were running around picking all my pieces up for me. I felt like the scarecrow in *The Wizard of Oz*, my arms over here, my legs over there and my body in the bushes somewhere.

I was, indeed, a mess, and the trouble was I still didn't know how sick I was. How suicidal I was. I couldn't even stand to be in my own skin, and I had decided that I had messed up everything, and everybody's lives, big time.

Who was I to love now?

What man would ever love me? Who wanted me?

THOUGHTS OF SUICIDE began to creep up on me, and they were taking over now almost on a daily basis. In May of 2000 I wrote my first suicide letter. I was badly beaten down by life, and living with a closed mind. I was attached to the evil things that were being said to me, and done to me.

It was out of desperation that I called my ex-husband. I had begun seeing a shrink. He had led me down a path during the last session, that I truly missed my ex. That I was feeling guilty about the affair that I had started with the married predator.

The shrink had said that, "You should feel lucky that he is willing to take you back." And that his wanting to charge me rent to live back in his home was, "Part of the punishment for my behavior."

Talk about self-sabotage, and to think that I actually swallowed down that crock of shit! No wonder I threw-up.

A little tiny voice inside me was saying "NO" at the top of her lungs, but I had my fear, guilt and shame ear plugs in. I wasn't listening to Kathleen anymore.

Looking back now, with my 20/20 vision of course, I realize that the more I asked for help, the more I became helpless. The reason being was that I was using *their* ways to work out my challenges, and it just doesn't WORK, unless it is *your own* reasoning, and *your own* belief.

IN JULY OF 2000 I moved back in with my ex, thinking that the affair had been just something I needed to do. I doubted myself, and believed that worthless shrink and what he had said to me.

Who knows you better than you?

It was a great big fat mistake to listen to that shrink. You see, while I missed my daughter, Sarah, who had decided to reside with her dad, and all the pets too, I did not miss my ex at all.

I went back to live with the father of my children with my tail between my legs. And for someone who had taken years to muster up enough strength and courage to leave, I had gone back to him faster than the speed of light.

An agreement, actually a deal, was made that I would pay my ex $400.00 a month to live in the home where Sarah and he lived. I agreed to this, extremely confused and distraught.

I had no family support whatsoever, nobody to stand up for me. I was very alone in the world, or so it felt at the time. Imagine, feeling like the only person you felt you could turn to was the very person you just had the law help you get away from.

As days and weeks passed, I tried to pretend that this would be my new life. That this was what I really wanted, and oh, how I wanted someone to just love me, to hold me forever, and make all the pain go away.

It was convenient for sure to be living there, compared to where I had been. My summer job was only 10 minutes away. I was in a house, not in an apartment, and I could run trails and the roads in this country setting. What more could I ask for? So Kathleen, just get on with it. Be grateful that he has forgiven you, and move on, girl. You are a sinner, and you need to repent, win his love back.

I was falling down deeper into the black hole, deeper into the depths of unconsciousness.

I MANAGED TO make it through most of the summer. Then, there came this gnawing feeling that would not let me go. I felt like I missed the predator, but I wasn't sure.

I decided to go back to the gym that we had attended together. I had promised my ex that I would not go back there, but these strong feelings, these desires were taking over, and they needed to be satisfied! I thought that facing him would be the test to see if I was in fact OVER him. I went back to the yoga classes that we had taken together. Hoping, even praying that I would see him. Still attracted to the drama, the shit!

Yes, there he was, and as he entered in through the workout center's doors, I was his once again.

We began spending time together, running and biking, and then the sex started. The lewd, crude sexual acts, doing them just to please him, and creating an illusion that this was in fact love. Yes, love.

I think it was the closeness, the contact of human touch that was the real need for me, what I really wanted.

Within a few weeks, the affair was full blown, two addictive personalities reunited once again. Once again, I was living two lives, living lies.

I had decided to go down with this ship, this nightmare, and it almost cost me my life.

SIXTEEN

IN SEPTEMBER OF 2000, Labor Day weekend, it was the grand finale at my summer position. I was unable to keep a visiting date with my father. There was an overlap of jobs, as my summer job was ending, the fall position had begun. Since I was living and working on the outskirts of Manchester, I wasn't able to visit as often as I would have liked to.

Finally, on the Tuesday evening after Labor Day, I went over to my dad's home to touch base with him. When I got to my dad's house it was early afternoon. I knocked on the door. There was no answer. He was probably out walking. So, I decided to finish up some errands that I had to do, and I would stop by later on.

The next day I returned to my father's house at dusk. I knocked at the door and rang the doorbell several times. An unsettling feeling descended over me.

The first thing that came to my mind was that he was angry with me for not coming during the weekend, as I had said I would, and he wasn't coming to the door because he wanted to punish me.

Dad had never given my brother or I a key to his house. One of those rules of his you just complied with. He was our father after all, and we just didn't waste any energy on trying to change his mind, it was a given.

I agonized over what to do next, but learned behavior from the past of never, ever doing anything without his permission came back to me, and I was nine years old again, frozen. My mind was racing, my emotions already taxed to the limit.

Finally, I called my brother. I thought he would validate my grave concern, and in the name of my brother's love, I trusted his call on this. He said that Dad was probably just drinking, and very disappointed that I hadn't come over!

Well, I wasn't going to give up. So I decided to go around the house to look for a sign of anything, but came up with nothing. Then, I went back to the side entrance and opened up the aluminum storm door to the wooden door.

I pushed open the little door of the mail slot, put my ear to the small opening, hoping, no praying for some noise for my ear to catch!

Nothing!

Now, I began to slowly unravel. Frantically I called his name through the small mail opening.

"Dad," I said loudly, in a scared tone.

No response still!

"Dad, are you there? I'm sorry that I couldn't come over the other day, but I had to work!"

As I listened intently, the only sound was the sound of silence, and it was a terrifying sound at that moment. For now, I was seriously worried.

However, I was going to give it another try. So, once again I opened up the mail slot, and yelled into the opening. "Dad, are you there?"

All of a sudden, as I was bent down listening, my ear tightly pressed against the mail slot opening, I heard him! It was muffled, and sounded like an angry, drunken tone, a tone that resurrected memories of my childhood and adolescence.

It was so hard to understand what he was yelling, it was barely audible, but it sounded like, "Get out of here! Get out of here!" I was filled with mixed emotions. Ecstatic to hear Dad's voice, but so deeply saddened to think that I probably contributed to his going on a binge by not showing up for our scheduled visit.

I closed the mail slot door. I stepped back away from the wooden door, and then I closed the storm door. I went back to my truck and tried to compose myself, crying in disbelief, with the sound of my sobs echoing inside.

Once I was able, I called my brother from my cell phone. He tried to convince me that Dad was just really angry, and that he would be all right in a couple of days.

I listened, like he was the expert on situations like this, and went against the instinctive feeling I had to see my father. I drove back to my ex's, to his house, not *my* home, where my daughter was.

THE NEXT DAY, as I drove down the street where my dad lived, I noticed a police cruiser in front of the house, and my brother's car there too. A cold chill came over me. It was a moment forever frozen in time, and everything was in slow motion.

As I parked my pick-up truck, I noticed two policemen at the door. The glass of the door had been broken on the side door, facing east.

As I entered, my brother came forward to greet me. He didn't even have to say anything really, the look in his eyes was enough to let me know that something horrible had happened.

"Kathy, we just found Dad on the floor. He's unconscious, and the police have just called for an ambulance."

"NO, NO, OH MY GOD, NO," was my first response. The news hit me so hard, like a thousand knives piercing my already broken heart!

I rushed to his side, hoping that he would suddenly get up, just like all the other times, and everything would be fine. I knelt down bedside him on the wooden floor where he had collapsed. I took his hand, it was cool and clammy to the touch. I gently patted his forehead. He was barely breathing, but he was still alive.

"Dad, Dad," I called gently. "Dad, its Kathy, I'm here. I'm here." There was no response. Once again I tried to get him to open his eyes, or even speak.

"Dad, Dad, dear God, Dad."

By that time, the ambulance and EMT's had arrived. They came in with the stretcher and some medical equipment. We were then asked to step out of the bedroom, where he was lying on the floor, so they could take his vital signs and begin an IV.

As the EMT's were leaving with our father, a police officer

approached us. He wanted to know why we didn't have a key to our Dad's house, and why we didn't enter sooner. His questions elicited feelings of blame and guilt, as if we already didn't have enough on our minds, and in the name of love, I took in all the words of the insensitive officer, and became overcome with a deep sense of guilt and sorrow. I wept bitterly as we drove to Catholic Medical Center. "Dad, oh Dad, I am so very sorry! I am sorry Dad," I said to myself between quiet sobs and quick breaths.

THE REALITY SET in quickly as my brother and I walked into the waiting room of the hospital. We had contacted our uncle, he was Dad's brother-in-law and also in charge of my Dad's estate.

We embraced our uncle tightly when he arrived, hoping for some comfort, and that maybe, just maybe, he could make it all go away!

Shortly after, the emergency room nurse emerged and asked for the family of Joseph Rioux. The nurse calmly stated that our father had suffered a major stroke, and that there had been some brain damage and paralysis as well. She wanted to know if he had a living will.

My brother and I had no idea of anything he would want to have done for him. Other than a few discussions about having a military funeral, any information about his wishes regarding life support or not had never been shared. My uncle knew some things because he was the executor of the estate, but like us had no idea of his plans.

He said, "I'll go to the safety deposit box at the bank to see if it holds any answers for us."

Falling down, down, down, this was another blow on top of an already full plate for me.

DAD DID NOT have a living will, so it was the responsibility of the hospital to do all they could for our father. He was then placed into the CMC acute care rehabilitation program.

As days passed by, and the reality of his condition was understood by my brother and I, it became painful to visit our dad. The care given and all the staff members were so kind and compassionate. It's just that it wasn't Dad anymore. It just wasn't!

To see him in a wheelchair, unable to walk, to dress or even feed himself was so pitiful, and I hated that this had happened to him. The vision of my dad now was torturous. I did not want to come to the hospital, but I did though, as much as I could tolerate.

Soon after, I left my ex-husbands home, and I went to reside in Dad's empty home. It seemed more appropriate that I stay in Manchester for many reasons. First of all, it gave me a haven from my entire world and the people in it too!

Secondly, his home in Manchester was close to the hospital and to where I worked. Lastly, and most importantly, it gave me distance from the predator.

Oh, I had work and an art class I had signed up for at the Art Institute that worked as great distractions, but distractions are simply temporary fixes, Band-Aids if you will, to a life that was in desperate need of reconstructive surgery. Sooner or later everything, especially your past, catches up to you, and you have to face it so that you can be you.

BESIDES DEALING WITH the divorce issues, all of which I hadn't addressed, just stuffed, I now began to stuff my feelings of my dad's stroke. Meanwhile, the predator was back in my life, and a relative was extremely upset that I was living in my father's house!

The relative had made some claims about the legalities of it all. I had told a relative that I had no place to go, hoping I would elicit some kind of understanding, and he would back off on telling me to get out of my dad's home. Or, at the very least offer me a room in his lovely large home, but he never did.

My daughters at the time remained distant towards me, but they were just as confused as I was, I believe. I understand now, they couldn't give what they didn't have.

The odds of continued mental and physical well-being were slim, and often times I felt so alone, like I was screaming for help, but nobody could hear me, nobody cared to come.

In the Name of Love

DAYS AND WEEKS passed. The social worker at CMC met with my brother and I, and evidently Dad had gone through all the comprehensive therapy. The rehab program had done everything possible, and the time had come and gone for Dad to improve.

In November of 2000, we placed our dad at the Veterans' Nursing Home here in Manchester, NH. We had gone to many other facilities, and felt that this would be the best place for him to call home.

I went to the house, Dad's home, alone that evening. It was dark, and it was empty, even though it was filled with furniture. I was filled with grief, for I had lost my daddy, but he was still alive.

I went into the bedroom where we had found him. It smelled of urine. He couldn't even get up to go.

I kept reliving the horror of thinking that when he had been calling out that night he was not drunk, or angry, but he had been calling out for me to help him! I tried not to beat myself up too much. I told myself for comfort, "Kathy, you didn't know! You didn't know!"

Tears streamed down my cheeks. I closed the door to his bedroom, and went to lie down in the bed I had set up in the empty spare bedroom. I didn't even have the energy to undress, or get ready for bed. I just lay down on top of the covers. I cried myself to sleep wondering why this had to happen. Asking God for the strength to take this, just take it.

I did take it, and stuffed it, along with all the other feelings, all the other things that were being said to me, in the name of the love of those around me.

IT WAS NOVEMBER of 2000, the holidays were just around the corner. Fragile from all that I had allowed into my life, I decided that I would redesign the holidays. To celebrate Thanksgiving and Christmas in a whole new way!

The divorce had brought on another type of drama, like who would see whom, and when and where. It was such a waste of precious energy.

So, in order to spare myself all the pain again, I wouldn't be celebrating Thanksgiving in the traditional manner, I instead would go to visit my mom—who was up in the Glencliff Home for the elderly—the Sunday before Thanksgiving, and visit with Kristen, Sarah and family at another time.

I went to visit my mother, and the predator wanted to come. Reluctantly I agreed, that little tweak inside me saying, "Danger, danger, danger," but I silenced it with a self-sacrificing biscuit!

Things had changed with the predator, and I was allowing him to use words and actions that were crossing the line of disrespect. Red flags were flying, but I overlooked them because I thought I was responsible for his personal situation.

I was letting fear and guilt slowly take control.

The drive to Glenciff Nursing Home seemed like a cross-country road trip; instead of a few hours, it felt like a few days. That good old walking on eggshells kind of feeling from the past was back in full force!

Once we arrived, the "pred" decided that he wasn't going to come in, and that he would be waiting in his vehicle for me. I checked in at the nurse's station, just like I always had. The nurse told me that she would go get my mother, and for me to wait in the lounge.

As I waited for Mom for come, I managed to gaze out one of the windows, and I thought how lucky my mom was in some ways. No worries, or cares, and to be up here by Mt. Washington, with breathtaking views of other mountains in the Presidential Range. I tried to take in as much of the tonic as I could. I breathed in deeply once, then twice, hoping that my breath would erase all my worries and cares. The peaceful second was ended abruptly when the nurse returned to the room. She informed me that my mother did not want to see me, that she was too tired.

"WHAT?" I said to myself, as the words shot through my heart like a dozen arrows. I tried to hold back tears of disappointment. Then the guilt of not coming to see her regularly, and the fear that she would stay mad at me took over.

I began to plead with the nurse, actually beg her, into allowing me to see my mom. I swallowed my pride and told the nurse that I had come up here all the way from Manchester, and that I wouldn't be able to see my mother on Thanksgiving Day.

The nurse then rolled her eyes, and pointed to where my mom was. I think she thought I might cause a scene or something. "Your mother is in the TV room. You may go in for a very brief visit."

Mom seemed extremely distant, in a daze almost! Not friendly at all either, I hadn't seen this kind of behavior from her in a long, long time. With the onset of Dad's stroke, I had been preoccupied, and I had neglected to visit her as often as I used to. Needless to say, being in an already fragile state, I took this rejection from my mother very, very personally!

I talked small talk to my mother with the hope that it would spark up a conversation, but Mom just sat there in a large old overstuffed chair, expressionless, and she never even uttered a single word. Even after I told her that Dad had suffered a major stroke.

After about an hour or so of this one-way conversation, I decided that it was time to go. I could no longer continue on in this manner. So, I said, "Happy Thanksgiving Mom," and gave her a big hug and a kiss on the cheek. I got up from the chair and walked down the hallway to the EXIT door. Before opening the door, I turned to see my mom still sitting in the same place she'd been in. I yelled out to her, "I LOVE YOU," and waved good-bye.

If you could only know the future, and what was about to come into your life, you could probably better prepare yourself. Like the weather forecast prepares you for rain, so you can bring your umbrella. You could arm yourself with lots of love—warm fuzzies that would shield you from anything.

If you don't love yourself unconditionally, how can anyone else?

EARLY THE following Monday morning after visiting my mother, my cell phone rang. I picked up the receiver and said, "Hello?" The person on the other end was from the Glencliff Nursing Home.

"Hi Kathleen, so sorry to be calling you, and I did try to reach your brother last night, but...but..." There was a long uncomfortable silence on the other end of the line. "Your mother passed away last night in her sleep. She died of a heart attack. I am so very sorry that I had to be the one to tell you the news."

I immediately called my relatives while I still had the strength to do so. I was in shock. I didn't want the news to paralyze me yet, so I acted. The reaction would come soon enough.

It was very difficult for me to call my relatives. Our relationship over the past month or so had become estranged because they didn't want me living in my father's empty house. So, I kept the conversation brief, trying not to come unglued.

I called my daughters, Sarah and Kristen to let them know about their grandmother, and then I think I called a few of my very close friends too, still trying as hard as I could not to fall apart on the phone as I spoke.

Then, I called the place I worked to let them know I wouldn't be coming in until after Thanksgiving due to the death of my mother. The secretary took my message, and offered me her deepest sympathy. I put the receiver back down and lay down on the floor.

No place to run! No place to hide! The news had finally found me.

My mom died. My mom died. Another moment frozen in time, a moment when you can recall exactly where you were.

"MOM," I cried out!

I curled up in the fetal position on the cold wooden floor and wept bitterly for a mother I really never knew, but she was my mom, and I would miss her.

THE WAKE WAS to be at McGugh's Funeral Parlor, the very same place where my grandparents had been waked, and who knows, maybe other generations that had gone before. A tradition I guess, the funeral director being of Irish descent and all.

During the wake that evening, we had an unusual visitor. A long lost family member, someone I had never met before. We had heard of him, but we had never met him in person. It was our half-brother, Raymond.

Raymond was a gentle soul; he seemed lost, just as we all were, still looking for a break that would make it all right. We embraced Raymond, and welcomed him, for this was his mother, too! I was glad to finally meet him. He had been hidden from us because he was born out of wedlock. Like us, Ray was born into all the shit that wasn't his either.

THE FUNERAL MASS was held at Our Lady of Perpetual Help church, an appropriate place for Mom's final farewell. For, it was at this same church that she was married, and also the church where my brother and I were baptized.

As my brother and I arrived, Raymond was waiting for us. We had told him the night before that we wanted him to sit with us in the church, that we were all her children.

Raymond looked so fragile. I wanted to comfort him, but I couldn't. I didn't have anything left. I had lived up to all their dreams that had made me this way, and I was drowning!

So, my two brothers and I went down the main aisle that lead to the altar. There were more people in the church than I thought would be present. Candles were lit on the altar, and the priest was at the end of the aisle to greet us.

I went before the people in the church on that cold and bitter November day. I felt that there were things that needed to be said on her behalf. That I needed to SHOUT out that she was our mother, and that I was in fact, thankful that she was. Yes, even proud!

I stated that she had given me the greatest gift of all, MY LIFE, through her love of life. And that even though she had spent her life in an institution, about 40 long years, and had not raised the three of us, she had indeed taught us many lessons.

I was not ashamed that Dolores Rioux was my mother. I am grateful!

THE WEATHER WAS a little bitter, so the blessing of the body would be done in the mortuary. Most all the friends and family members that were at the mass attended the cemetery service.

The predator was at the opening to the mortuary waiting for me. He walked in with me, and waited by the coffin. As I stood there, who comes in but my ex-husband with our two daughters by his side.

There was no shortage of show-offs that day, for two of them were on either side of me. Not there for me, but for themselves!

My daughters didn't come over to where I was. Certainly, the predator had scared them away. They probably thought that I had chosen the predator over our family, and throughout the blessing given by the priest, I kept looking over towards them, hoping that they would give me some sign of hope that they still loved me. But they never did.

Being in the state of mind that I was in at the time, I mistook their behavior as a sign of great disapproval, that they were mad at me. Or worse, that my daughters hated me. In the name of love of my daughters, I blamed myself for their feelings.

Following tradition, we then proceeded to the Yard Restaurant, where we would provide a final farewell meal to those who were mourning our mother.

I waited and waited for my daughters to show up, but they did not come to the Yard Restaurant. Instead, their father had taken them to I believe Chez Vachon Restaurant, on Kelley Street, to have breakfast.

Of course, the girls not showing up was a wonderful opportunity for a manipulator/predator to use this situation to his advantage, and he said to me, "I am the only one here for you."

The predator told me that my daughters didn't want me, but the truth was that they were just confused. Nothing was calculated, they were just wounded, and their alienation became a weapon he could use to control this suicide romance!

The love/fear relationship I had with the predator was one of great familiarity. You see, everyone I loved growing up, with the exception of a few of my friends, I was also afraid of.

Being a Catholic I loved God, but I was also petrified of his wrath that the nuns and priests taught us. That if I disobeyed any of the commandments, I would go to hell. Love equaled fear. So, on an emotional level I was comfortable with having fear side by side with love. Pain and discomfort were the norm in my daily life as opposed to kindness and respect.

It was not on an intellectual level that I invited the predator into my world. I equated his attention, his compliments, his love for adventure and his rebellious spirit with love. He listened to me and I felt like I could confide in him. Things that my ex-husband hadn't done in years.

Soon he knew my whole story, which was to his advantage. Because, in the end all the things he knew would be used against me. I began to second guess myself, and he used the alienation of my family and would tell me, "Nobody is here for you but me."

The manipulation, evil controlling and isolation had me relying on him totally. He had me believing that he was all I had. I couldn't leave because I thought I wouldn't have anyone else. The PTSD I was suffering from had triggered my deep fear of abandonment.

Love can motivate and paralyze you, so can fear!

The red flags had been flying, but I had never taken heed to them. I just couldn't. I was very sick mentally and physically, powerless to function. I didn't even know how sick I was, but the predator knew. He knew it, and would use it to his advantage! And when he offered to bring me away up north, away from all of this, I agreed. In the name of love of the predator, I went.

It was a decision that would haunt me for a long, long time.

And the Thunder Moon waned.

SEVENTEEN

I HAD GONE back to my dad's house in Manchester, where I had been residing since his stroke in September. The predator had said that he would pick me up there after he had gone back to his place in Hooksett, NH.

Although, he might as well have called my father's house his, for he had been coming there so often! I had never even asked him to stay. He just came, and I never dared to say that he couldn't.

I couldn't put my finger on it, but there was an intense feeling inside me, gnawing at me in fact, to not go away with the predator. His words and actions of late had crossed over that already lowered line of what I would tolerate or accept from anyone. But honestly, I just didn't have the strength to see the real truth and to muster up the courage and say, "NO THANKS!"

Once again, I was concerned with his feelings, and how thoughtful it was of him to want to take me away. His approval was worth more to me than I was worth to myself. Our destination was to be Lincoln, NH. We had discussed skiing on Thanksgiving, instead of doing the traditional family celebration. He had been more or less outcast by his family also, and had no plans.

He would say, "My family are a bunch of assholes," and go on and on. They were the ones with all the problems, never him, and I would listen, I had better!

YOU COULD CUT the tension with a knife as we drove north, the predator and I. He was very, very angry about my family's reaction to him. He reminded me time and time again that they didn't care about me. That I was just like my mother.

"Remember, your mom got involved with a married man, too!"

All the emotional blackmail worked like a charm. My family's reactions had already spoken to me. Their words and actions were ones of disapproval. I felt like I didn't have anyone except for the predator.

As we drove along the interstate, he kept on insisting that I drink this pink colored concoction that he had made in a water bottle. The water bottle was a frosted one, with its contents filled to the top. It tasted fruity, and I was thirsty at the time, so I drank it down. I was so grateful that he had thought to bring something for me to drink.

Halfway there I began to feel odd. My head began to spin.

I felt like I weighed a ton.

I felt lethargic, and began to sweat profusely.

I told the predator how I was feeling, and his reaction was like he could not have cared less, like I was a bother. He was distant, cold and cruel, undaunted by my condition as he said, "So what?"

Another blow for me, as his words hit me like a sword, penetrating to my heart, but whatever he had given me, drugged me with, had dulled the effect.

When we finally arrived in Lincoln, we drove down the road until we came to an Inn there. We pulled into the parking lot, and the predator said he would go in to check to see if they had any vacancies.

I was so glad when he got out of the vehicle. I was feeling really poorly, and it gave me a chance to relax a little. I felt terrible in a way that I had never, ever felt before. What was wrong with me?

The predator left his cell phone in the vehicle. I stared at it, tempted to use it, to have someone come and get me. But the thought passed quickly, as I asked myself, "Who would come? Who?" And I answered my own question, "Probably nobody."

I unfortunately dismissed it as part of all that this day had brought to me. The funeral of my mother, meeting my half-brother and still feeling so empty, abandoned, by my dad's stroke. I felt just like a truck had hit me when, in actuality, it was life that had hit me. Several times already that year. My body, however, was trying to tell me something else, but I wasn't listening!

I couldn't even cry anymore; I was all out of tears.

Then, the door swung open. It was the predator returning from the Inn. He told me to get my suitcase. It was an order, even though he knew that I wasn't feeling well. It made little difference to him. He didn't offer to help me, and the tone of his voice told me not to even ask him to carry my suitcase in for me.

We went to the front desk together. We checked in, with my credit card. I was hoping to smooth things over and wipe out the frigid temperature coming from the man next to me. I felt like I was with a total stranger. I could feel all his anger, all his frustrations. Like a volcano, just waiting to erupt!

THERE WAS NO bellhop to take our luggage up to the room for us—just the time when I really could have used the help. I was getting weaker by the minute. I hoped that I would be able to make it up to our room without passing out.

His silence was deafening! I followed anxiously, uncertain now of what was to come. I felt like a sheep, trusting someone dressed in sheepskin. Walking on eggshells. Oh, so familiar.

He led the way. I followed in silence, barely able to walk now, let alone carry on a conversation. Just hoping to make it to the room where I could just lay down and rest.

Sleep. Yes, just to sleep. Shut out the whole world for a little while. I sighed once we finally reached the door to our room. He placed the key into the keyhole and swung the door open. He entered first, I followed closely behind, staggering now, bag and baggage.

It was a regular size room, with two double beds. The beds each had a maroon quilted bedspread. There was a nightstand between the two beds. Across from the beds was a maple dresser with a mirror. Beside the dresser was another cabinet, complete with a television and stereo system.

It looked so inviting, especially the beds. I put my luggage down beside the bed closest to the door, and collapsed on that bed. He put his bag down beside my things as well, and began to tell me what HE had planned for US that evening.

"You are mine tonight," he said, in a manner that reminded me of Hannibal Lecter. I could barely speak. I felt so weak, so sick, but I managed to utter my weak response to his command. And in a barely audible voice, in a sound just above a whisper, I said, "NO, I can't. I just buried my mother. I'm so sick, I need to rest."

The slamming of the door resonated throughout the room, a signal that the hellish nightmare had begun.

"What," he demanded, "do you think I brought you up here for?"

I couldn't run! I couldn't hide!

I became a victim of circumstance, and I hated the predator, but I hated myself even more for trusting him. For on that night, I got something I didn't ask for, and I was wrong for letting fear, guilt and shame control me.

I would never be the same, NEVER!

It was like history was repeating itself, and I felt like I had become just like my mom.

WHEN PREDATORS ATTACK their prey, they do so when their prey is at a most vulnerable point. They do this so that they can attack, and get what they want, without too much of a struggle.

On November 22, 2000, I was at a very low point, a prey point. I was without any ability whatsoever to struggle, or defend myself. There was a bitter chill in the air, in that room. I could feel the predator's evil.

My mind was racing. The anticipation was consuming me as I tried to figure out just what his plan was for me. *Please God, please let someone come to get me. Kristen, Sarah, my family, anybody! I am here, in this Inn, in Lincoln, NH. Please come, take me somewhere, anywhere, but here!* I screamed inside, to myself, my message never to be heard by anyone.

"No, no, no," I said to him again, just above a whisper. I was semiconscious, drugged by whatever he had slipped into my water bottle. He then came toward me and felt my forehead. I was sweating profusely, and shivering and shaking uncontrollably. I had never, ever experienced anything like that before. But my condition did not stop the predator from continuing.

He roughly removed all my clothes, piece by piece, as I lay on the bed, not to help me of course, but so that he could help himself to my body. I couldn't even stop him from undressing me, for now I was shaking even more, having difficulty breathing. I believe I was nearly in shock.

He did this to me, because he could, and I couldn't fight back. The effects of the drug were overwhelming; my brain could not process this horrific event, and I lost all consciousness for a while.

I awoke later, I don't recall how long I was out, to him on top of me groping me breasts, holding them hard, and sucking on the nipples, going from one breast to the other. Then he moved down, roughly pushing my legs apart so that he could go down on me, my legs pinned down by his upper body. He was ravenous, like a hyena that hadn't eaten for weeks. The darkness in him was exposed totally for the first time, consuming me.

"You like this, you bitch. Nobody wants you. Nobody! Not even your children! I want you though," he said to me. "I want you for sex. Sex is good for you," he told me in a commanding voice.

I was like a rag doll, as once again I begged him, "No, I can't. I can't."

My words were ignored as he continued to fuck me all over, mentally and physically. Rape and sexual assault seem like such inadequate words to describe the hellish ordeal I experienced.

THE ROUGH GROPING and grasping of my breasts, buttocks and thighs continued on. Then he thrust his index finger into my vagina. It hurt so much, the pain was excruciating, as I felt some of the flesh inside me being torn away. I was still shaking uncontrollably, semi-conscious, begging, no praying, for unconsciousness to take me over.

I couldn't fight him off; I couldn't even speak now, as I surrendered my body to the devil, the predator. But not my spirit, NEVER!

He tried to have intercourse with me, the semi- conscious woman, Kathleen, but I was too dry. He forced his penis into me, tearing yet more of my vaginal area.

"Please don't," I said with one last breath, hoping there was a speck of decency left somewhere floating around inside him, but there wasn't. His silky words and actions of the past didn't match up to this, and as I slipped into unconsciousness, I thought to myself, "It was so much easier before you became you."

"Drink this," the predator demanded, and as I came to, he pulled me up forcefully to sit-up, but I couldn't. He then roughly pushed the water bottle to my lips and poured the liquid into my mouth, leaving me to swallow some, and choking on the rest.

He turned my limp body over, exposing my naked backside, and the humiliation was torture as he pulled up my buttocks to have anal sex with me. He roughly gripped my thighs to keep my body at the right angle for his sexual assault, but couldn't get himself hard enough to enter. He let go of me, and my body made the bed bounce when I landed.

I was still awake, unfortunately, as I could hear him masturbating behind me, the noise of skin against skin. He was mumbling to himself, "Come on, come on."

Unsuccessful at his attempt to come, the predator then laid down on the bed and pulled me on top of him, his front to my back, placing his penis between my buttocks, hoping that it would arouse him enough so that he could get off.

At this point, I remember saying to myself, "Dear God, why is this happening to me? Why? Please give me the strength to get through this. Oh God, where are you?"

Once again I was brought back to reality by violent shaking and a hard smash to my face.

"Drink this," he commanded, and I did. I sipped the liquid; I didn't dare not to. I was afraid there would be more to take from him.

His hands groped me all over again, as he was still under me with me on top, in a sitting position. He was again attempting anal sex with me. Pushing and pushing until he finally penetrated as he thrust his penis inside me. I was so sickened by this action that I vomited all over myself. It was just a small amount of fluid, as I hadn't had much to eat that whole day.

The predator rose quickly, pushing me off him roughly, just like you'd toss a rag doll. Then his anger flared as he yelled, "For God sake you fucking bitch, couldn't you have told me that you were going to be sick? Now look what you've done," his loud voice unable to penetrate through the drugs and sexual assaults, because Kathleen wasn't there, she had slipped into an unconscious state again, thank God!

BY THE TIME I woke up, the vomit had been cleaned up. The wretched smell hit my nostrils, and I almost lost it again, but there was nothing left in me, I had the dry heaves.

I had stirred once again because his hands were groping my body, mostly my breasts, and he was performing oral sex on me. I was just an object to him now, a toy, and he had absolute power, and I believed it.

All through the night he would wake me and command me to drink the concoction in the water bottle. Then climb on top of me again to quench his sexual appetite.

And just when I thought the worst was over, I visited hell on earth.

I was on my back now, my arms to my side and my legs spread apart. He was on the bed kneeling down between my legs. When I was able to focus better, I could see that he was masturbating again. Rubbing his penis with one hand and holding it with the other. It was a repulsive act.

When he became hard, he crawled up toward my head, sitting on my chest. His weight pushed on my rib cage, and my breath became harder to take in. He then kneeled down using his legs to hold my arms down. The prey, Kathleen, was trapped by the predator. Then he took his hard penis and forced in into my mouth, as far down as it would go.

I couldn't breathe, I couldn't get him off me, and at this point I thought I was going to suffocate!

"Come on, come on, suck on my dick, you bitch."

When I was unable to accommodate his request, he began to move his penis up and down inside my mouth until he came.

"Oh my god, no, oh God can you hear me?"

When I began to choke, and gasp for air, he finally pulled himself off.

I shut down all my emotions. I had to feel nothing, because on that night, the predator had eaten his prey. He had devoured my body, my mind, but not my soul.

I got something from the predator that I never, ever asked for.

EIGHTEEN

LIFE HAD REALLY beaten me up. My divorce, my father's stroke and my mother's death were overwhelming enough. However, it was the relationship with the predator that did the most catastrophic damage.

From November 2000 on I lost myself almost completely. I was now the personal sex slave to the predator. I didn't even dare say he was raping me. I merely referred to the rapes as "sex on demand," which was a major denial of what was taking place.

I had tried desperately to get help from my family. Phone conversations telling then some of the torrid details of his actions, but they would dismiss them because they didn't want to believe them, they couldn't, because then it would be true, and they would have to get involved.

I was screaming at the top of my lungs for someone to save me, but nobody heard me, they didn't even seem to care. My family couldn't give what they didn't have, unconditional love.

I was severely unwell, both physically and mentally. Thoughts of suicide now occurred on a daily basis. The trauma of the sexual assaults and the eating disorder, all of it was taking their toll on me.

I should have been hospitalized. I should have. The predator knew how ill I was, but the predator never gives up his prey.

IN DECEMBER I resigned from my position at my job. I knew that my days were numbered, as I could barely function. I was trying as best as I could to hide my fear of living my life with the predator. I was addicted to him now. Brainwashed to believe that he was the only one there for me, not realizing that the relationship was lethal!

In the middle of December I took the worst step of my life—I moved in with the predator. I had no other place to go to, and he knew it. He knew about my past, he knew about the eating disorder. He could chew me up and spit me out easily, without any confrontation.

I was barely breathing from the drugs he was giving to me, I believe, and his continued sexual exploitations. My days were like living in a fog; I existed in a robot-like fashion. I was keeping hardly any food down, but I really think that the food represented my current life crisis, and when I threw up, I was simply getting rid of all the shit that I had been force fed. Like a survival technique! I was like an alcoholic, or drug addict. No one ever wants to grow up to become one, it just happens.

Things were quite tumultuous at this time. Crazy, I mean crazy! I don't even remember Christmas Day. Who I was with, or where I was. I do recall finding out that he had been reading my diary. It had been moved and the bookmark I used to mark the place where I had last written was on the floor, beside the bed. I could just imagine it now, the predator reading my diary over and over again for his personal entertainment. "Yes!" I can hear him tell himself, as he collected more information to destroy me with, to succeed at emotional blackmail.

You see, the predator needed facts, so that he could take control, benefit his needs, his wants, and he certainly had a great big pile of trump cards now! He had control over me totally, just like a drug, and my addiction to him was killing me.

Months, weeks, days and hours passed by and I had no power to leave. The predator had it all, like a bloodsucker, he had drained almost every ounce of hope from me.

IN JANUARY OF 2001 I went to McGugh's Funeral Parlor to plan my funeral. It was only appropriate that they do the honors—you know, family tradition and all.

What family? Why did I want to still have their approval even at death?

Anyway, I planned the whole thing with Kevin McGugh, the owner. I mean even the detail of my body being cremated, and that my ashes where to be sprinkled over Mt. Washington, the first mountain that I had ever climbed.

There would be bagpipes at the church to play "I'll Take You Home Again, Kathleen," a song I loved, one that brought me peace every time I listened to it. Because I wanted to be far away from this terrible, horrible place, and all the terrible people in it!

I had planned to overdose on sleeping pills and alcohol. It would be quick, and I wouldn't be a bother to anyone. I mean, if I had a breakdown like my mother, then I'd be a bother. I couldn't bear the thought of my children having to come visit me in that kind of condition, or in an institution.

So, I wanted to die. I wasn't afraid of death, wasn't afraid that the predator would kill me. I was afraid that he would keep me alive so that he could rape me every single day. Fuck me OVER, and OVER and OVER again!

All I could manage to think about at the time was a roof over my head, and a place to have my belongings in. It didn't matter to me anymore who I was with, because soon it would be all over. I had numbed myself from the daily verbal abuse and sexual assaults. I was in the war zone now, right in the front line of attack, and I was shell-shocked. I was addicted to the very drug that was killing me.

All that was left of me was my things. Kathleen was temporarily out of commission.

FOUNDATIONS MADE OF clay cannot withstand the complexities of living, and the choices we make are made from what we know. If we don't know better, we can find ourselves living in grass huts, instead of the mansions we all deserve!

My grass hut certainly had guilt, fear, shame and the predator living in it. There wasn't any room for anyone else. My daughters were distant and aloof, trying to deal with the divorce and my living in the grass hut and all. The predator didn't want my daughters visiting while he was home, and he would seize every opportunity he could to say, "See?

Your daughters don't care about you anymore. They don't come to visit you, even when I'm not here."

However, I was too sick to realize that they didn't come around because they didn't like the predator, not me. Their behavior, in my mind, only validated my own sense of worthlessness from long ago, now fully resurfaced and heightened by the toxic relationship with him.

In April 2001 a typical day included waking to the predator pulling down my underpants, it could be two, three, maybe even four o'clock in the morning. It could be anytime, because time didn't matter anymore to him. I was there for the taking whenever he wanted.

I was terrified as I woke to the horror of the predator using his arms to hold down my legs, after first spreading them, and then having oral sex without my consent.

He would then proceed to grope my breasts, pulling on them really hard, and then sucking on the nipples until I was in excruciating pain, but I didn't dare utter a sound, or try to fight him off. No strength, and the fear that he would beat the living shit out of me.

"Nobody wants you. You are just like you mother. You turned out just like her. I want you, though. I want to fuck you as many times as I want to. You are so lucky you still have me." He would say it in a silky, sinister fashion.

I had given the predator my love, and he in turn had given me a passport to HELL!

Sometimes he would play with himself and then come all over my breasts and stomach, then use his hands to smear it around. Just like an animal, leaving behind his semen trail.

The assaults often lasted hours as he had a hard time getting aroused enough to come. When he was done with me, he would smirk and with an evil laugh and say, "I'm all set for a while." He would then get ready for work. He would shower, then have breakfast and prepare his lunch, as I lay in the bed FROZEN, not daring to move. No words, no stirring, no coughing, nothing.

"Just be still so he'll go away," I would tell myself.

Once, to my horror he came back and smashed me across the back, and said I needed to get help for the eating disorder, or he would call my family. What a wonderful expression of love and tenderness.

I was in a fog. I would sleep until noon, get up, eat, gorge myself, and then throw it all up. Shower, eat again, and keep some of the food down. I would try to read, but I really didn't have the strength to, and sadly I would fall asleep again.

Some days were a little better than others, as I would go to meet my friends for lunch. The shame and the guilt of the relationship never permitted me to divulge the truth of it. I would merely carry on, pretending that it was good.

Every now and then, I would break down and cry uncontrollably in front of my friends at one of our meetings, but would dismiss it as being upset over the divorce or my daughters not getting in touch with me.

On other days I would get to visit with my youngest daughter, Sarah. She lived closer to me than her older sister, so it was just a matter of convenience. I loved our visits, but the tension of all the mess was still present. We both were treading water, neither one able to save the other.

I did get to see Kristen, but it seemed only when all three of us could visit. It didn't matter what we did. My daughters were my lifelines, and like the air, I needed some contact with them. Even a once a month get together kept me going!

Later on during the day, I would return home. Eat again, gorge myself and throw everything up. It actually felt good to get rid of all the contents of my stomach. I was in survival mode, preparing for the big bad wolf's return.

I would then lie down on the couch, the bed or sometimes on the floor while watching a television program and pass out. I made sure that the alarm would be set for ten or fifteen minutes before 5pm so I could begin preparing dinner for him.

Evenings were uncomfortable and exhausting, as I hoped he would be too tired to verbally or sexually assault me. I behaved so nicely with my fake smile, and attentiveness, so maybe, just maybe, he would let me be.

And now fear, guilt and shame controlled me, and I was too far gone to love Kathleen.

IN MAY OF 2001 there was a new twist in the struggle with the predator. He was demanding that I go see a counselor for my problems. For MY PROBLEMS! It's almost amusing in hindsight. I mean who was the sick one, really?

My friend Lynn, who knew most of what was going on between the predator and I, suggested that I go see the counselor that she was seeing. She recognized the fear and shame I had, and thought that her counselor, Dr. K, might be of help to me. Unknown to me at that time, Lynn had been repeatedly raped in a close relationship.

Reluctantly, I made the appointment, just to quiet the monster I was living with. I figured that as long as I admitted that I needed the help, he would be satisfied, and the assaults would decrease.

So, when he returned from work one evening in May, I told the predator that I had made an appointment with Dr. K.

"Good," he said. "You know you really need the help," and for the time being he was satisfied. It might be for the evening, for a few hours or a few minutes that I could have some peace.

By then it seemed to me that the damage done was beyond repair. However, I went to see Dr. K. For the eating disorder, mind you, and not for the destructive relationship. The first few words out of his mouth were that he had in fact worked with my mother in Concord, and said, "I feel sorry for you that Dolores was your mother."

I thought to myself as the words spewed from his lips, "How dare you put down my defenseless mother, you condescending piece of shit?! I feel sorry that she had the misfortune of having you as her counselor." And within a matter of one session with this baboon, I had no respect for him, or what he said. However, I continued on with the weekly sessions to please the predator.

In hindsight, it seemed that the more I asked for help from those around me, the more I became helpless. I had the answers for me, no one else did, and I will never give anyone that power again!

EVERY SO OFTEN I would catch a glimpse of the Kathleen I used to be. The one that would have never tolerated the behavior of a son of a bitch like the predator, but she would disappear into the depths of my subconscious mind, and fear would win out.

I had thought about leaving many times, but now I didn't believe in myself anymore. Kathleen was lost months ago. I was truly out of my mind, and I didn't want to live anymore. Hopelessness and desperation were my new best friends. Had I, in fact, become just like my mother?

On June 9, 2001 I woke once again pinned underneath his body, my nightshirt raised up around my neck. He was rubbing my breasts really hard, and then he began to suck and bite down on the nipples. He then flipped my body over and pulled my legs down until they hung over the side of the bed.

Earlier, after removing my underpants, he had shoved his index finger and middle fingers into my vagina to find that I was too dry to have intercourse vaginally. He then placed two fingers into my rectum to find the lubrication necessary to enter my frail body, and then he brutally sodomized me.

"Oh my god was that good. Until we meet again," he sickeningly uttered, then laughed as he went toward the bathroom. As I heard the door slam shut, something inside me snapped, and I was filled with rage for the first time in memory. The petrified little cat in the corner had had enough, and she was going to stand up for herself now.

I dragged my battered body back up to my side of the bed, blood dripping onto the sheets from the forced entry into my rectum. Bite marks lightly visible on my left breast, and I stayed very still waiting to hear the shower curtain close. I knew he would be in there awhile. He usually spent a half hour or more pampering himself with his special soaps and shampoos. I guess he was trying to wash all the demons away. Then, with all the strength I could muster up, I got up from the bed to dress myself. My clothes still scattered on the floor from the night before.

First, I grabbed a tissue from the box on the bedside table to wipe the blood still dripping from me. I was barely breathing, and numb, as I focused on getting myself out of there, and not on any pain that my body was experiencing.

Then, I put on the underpants he had taken off me without permission, then my bra. Next came my shorts and a top. Then I quickly slipped into my sandals, and as I exited the bedroom I grabbed my pocketbook and keys with a clean sweep of my right hand.

I ran to my car, swung open the door and got in. I locked the doors just in case the predator had discovered my absence and was behind me. I placed the key into the ignition, put the truck into reverse, and headed to someone who I could trust totally, and who would take me in, no questions asked.

MY DESTINATION WAS to Rimmon Street, in Manchester. It was where my friend Lynn lived. Luckily for me she was at home when I arrived.

I told her everything that had just happened, and she held me as I became unglued in her tiny two-bedroom apartment. It was a no judgment zone. I could be sure that she wouldn't say that I wasn't smart enough, or pretty enough, or working hard enough to find myself in this situation, this HELL.

Lynn was helpful, but her plate was already full with her personal life and her job, and she couldn't give what *she* didn't have, either. However, I was so grateful to her for being there for me.

Everything seemed to be spinning wildly out of control. When you've always lived your life with secrets and lies, the TRUTH is almost impossible to deal with, and sometimes you would rather die than to face up to it. But sooner or later it does catch you, and when it does, you hit the ground!

Lynn wanted to go directly to the police department. I hesitated at first, because I felt like this was my problem and I could handle it.

Then, I had a flashback of the last incident. This had to stop! The predator had gone too far, and now it was time to get help from the authorities. Our next destination would be the Goffstown Police Department.

Still, something inside me was unsettled. The trouble with asking for help is that I had believed that it made you helpless, and you were a victim. I would now be relying on others to make decisions for me, and it was something I had never, ever believed in. But I was really too sick to know what I believed in anymore.

THE OFFICER AT the Police station was very compassionate and understanding. He gave me some comfort in the fact that the law would be involved now. He sat down with me to discuss what had been going on, and what had transpired today.

He told me that I would be filling out a restraining order. That it would be a temporary one, and that I would have to go back to court to finalize it.

He handed me the papers and left me in this little room to complete them. Lynn had stepped outside the room while I attempted to write the report.

I stared at the papers that were in front of me for a long time in disbelief. They were as intimidating as the relationship I had been part of, and the thought of writing down the truth of the past seven months or so meant telling that truth. Uncovering the secrets and all the lies, and I couldn't, I just couldn't!

It meant that I would have to face what I had just been through, and I wasn't really ready, mentally. It was all too much. What could I say? What was I willing to share? This would be read by many people, and I had to be careful, very careful.

The truth was that whatever I wrote down, I would be dealing with the aftermath, and in some part of me even wanted to protect the predator from harm. GO FIGURE!

After all he had done to me, I was still willing to turn the other cheek. The trouble was I had no more cheeks left, but I was still an approval prostitute. If I wrote or said unkind things, even if they were true, someone might not like me!

Well, I finally completed the report. It was definitely vague. It was only the tip of the iceberg—the small, teeny, tiny part that sticks out just enough for you to see. I gave just enough information for the law to keep him away from me, and yet not the whole truth. I had learned from my family how to hide the truth.

I handed the officer the report, at which time he informed me that he would accompany me to the apartment complex. He would enter first, and I would wait outside until he signaled it was safe for me to enter. I would then have fifteen minutes to gather whatever I could. Then I would be let out, and would not be allowed to come back for the remainder of my belongings until I had hired, HIRED an officer!

Fifteen minutes! Fifteen minutes! I couldn't believe it.

Then, I was told that I could call back on Tuesday and arrange to get the rest of my things. I would have to pay, PAY, an officer out of my pocket for a minimum of FOUR HOURS, even if it only took less than that. All the information given to me was overwhelming. I guess if you don't control your own life, someone else will.

Falling, falling down, down, down.

I WENT BACK to the apartment accompanied by a police officer and Lynn. The officer did as he had told me. First, he went in to make sure it was safe to go in. Then within a few minutes, he signaled for Lynn and me to enter.

The apartment was vacant. The predator wasn't anywhere to be found, which made the retrieval of some of my possessions easier. I was so relieved because I wasn't sure how he would have responded to a confrontation.

"Remember you have only fifteen minutes to gather what you need," the officer stated once again as we entered the apartment.

"Is this the main entrance?"

"Yes it is, officer," I said.

"Then I'll wait outside here in case he returns," the officer stated in a monotone manner, devoid of any emotion. He had probably done this many times before.

"Let's see. What do I take? What do I need?" Talking to myself now, my mind spinning wildly out of control.

Fifteen minutes.

I'm sure someone, somewhere, had decided that was ample time. Probably someone who never had to deal with a domestic violence incident! So, in refugee mode, all the essentials such as clothing, toiletries and treasured pictures were gathered together and placed into pillowcases and garbage bags, and I fled to safety.

LIKE A MISPLACED person, I went to Lynn's second floor apartment. She was kind enough to take me in. She graciously told me that I could settle into the spare bedroom to the right of the stairway.

As I sat down on the bed, I was consumed with despair. All I could see were the two garbage bags and the two pillowcases of things—my things—and I was reminded that in the name of love of the predator, this is what I had been reduced to.

There was a great uneasy force inside me, and even though I was at Lynn's home, I still did not have a sense of peace. I stared at the four bags of my things on the floor and I was terribly overcome with shock and horror. What had become of Kathleen?

That night was one of the hottest of the year. Lynn had invited some girl friends over for support, and we were going to spend the evening out together. We would first go to an outdoor concert at Singer Park, here in Manchester. Then head off to the Uptown Tavern for some dancing. As I dressed for the celebration, sweat poured off my forehead, and I stood in front of the fan to dry my body before putting on my pants and shirt. I couldn't really feel anything on the inside or out; only the sweat could be seen. I almost hit the ground.

In slow motion, I went out with Lynn and her friends. Some of them shared their own personal war stories, relationships gone crazy. One woman told the story of how her ex-husband had taken a baseball bat to her head and fractured her skull when she tried leaving him!

Then he had gotten off because the charges were dropped, I don't recall why.

Another had a similar story of abuse, with a similar outcome. I was simply horrified.

As they told their tales, I could not help but wonder what would be my outcome, my story. I was unraveling, like a ball of yarn that accidentally falls off the couch when you're making a scarf. I was now a warrior without any war to fight anymore. I was in shut-down mode, because that's what you do in order to survive the battlefield.

The shell-shocked Kathleen was facing her truth: that she had been sexually assaulted, raped, and it was terrifying being on the outside.

IT WAS A night filled with men bashing. Hair raising stories that would have been better off left unsaid, considering the state of mind I was in. The men were to BLAME and we were the victims, and now I was one of them, and I HATED that! The night of celebration turned out to be a nightmare.

I couldn't sleep as my mind kept rewinding the stories told to me earlier, abusive men who were NOT held accountable. Over and over and over again and the stifling heat of the night made me restless and full of rage. I whispered to myself:

"You told on him. You did, and now he is going to come and get you! He'll rape you again, and again and again. Then you'll end up just like your mother, a burden to everyone."

I quietly cried myself to sleep on that hot, humid evening, I vowed to get back all my things and bring them here, so that the predator wouldn't have them, and then, then there would be a death—my suicide, mine.

Hush now, hush now, it's almost over.

And the Thunder Moon waned.

NINETEEN

THE NEXT DAY was so foggy, pretty much a blur. I probably got up. I think I went for a walk. I know I ate and threw up at least a few times. Everything else is just a mystery.

The evening offered no relief, either. It was just as hot and humid as all the nights before. There wasn't even a breeze, and the fan was merely blowing around all the hot air in my room. I hadn't kept down any food in about two days, and I was going on my second night without sleep.

My newfound freedom didn't offer me any solace at all. I had no idea what to do with it. I wasn't free on the inside, which is where it matters the most.

I tried to get comfortable, but couldn't. I ended up going outside on Lynn's porch, where I found a lounge chair that was unoccupied. It was a little better outside. Probably a few degrees cooler than inside, and I fell asleep sometime the next day in the early morning hours.

My light was fading out by the minute now. For in the name of loving others, there was no one left to love. I couldn't love myself because there wasn't much left to love.

Besides the eating disorder, I was also suffering from vaginal bleeding. A condition which had plagued me on and off for the last six months. Sometimes the bleeding would last for up to ten days.

A meltdown, totally, of the mental element controlling the body, and my body had been screaming at me to leave the asshole, the predator. It had been telling me to remove myself from this tumultuous relationship a long, long time ago. Unfortunately, I didn't listen!

MONDAY MORNING SEEMED like it would never come. I was ready to get the rest of my belongings back. Everything I had was in that apartment we had shared, and being in the state of shock that I was in, those THINGS had become me. They were all that were left of Kathleen.

I went on this day to see Dr. K, the counselor I had seen for the eating disorder. I was vague in my confession of the relationship with the predator. I was so filled with fear, guilt and shame. Even though I had every reason to tell someone that I been drugged and raped, almost on a daily basis.

As I left the building where Dr. K was, I did not feel relieved, and instead was more afraid than ever! Now I had to face what had happened, and it was terrifying, simply terrifying.

I ate and ate. Then threw up and threw up some more.

I called my daughters and chatted with them. Disguising my voice, trying to sound composed, holding back tears and the truth, denying myself the right to feel the torment I had experienced.

THE NIGHT BEFORE had not provided me with a restful sleep, the intense heat had added to an already flammable situation. Today was Tuesday, the day that the Goffstown PD had promised me that I would be able to get the rest of my things.

I had called my brother before to ask his assistance in the removal of all of the rest of my worldly possessions. Things that were my treasures, like pictures, Christmas ornaments that my daughters had made, books and many other sentimental items.

I could not leave them behind in the predator's hands. He had taken me, and I would not allow him to take my belongings, too! My brain and body were confused, desperate, and my mind latched on to strange ideas.

First thing I did that morning was to call the Goffstown PD. When I finally got through, they casually informed me that they could NOT help me today.

"We're busy today, but we might be able to get your things on Friday," the officer on the other end of the receiver stated. "Try the Sheriff's Department, they do things like that, they might be able to help you."

It felt like another blow to me! I couldn't believe what I was hearing. I trusted them! I believed in them. This had been the first time I had ever asked for help, and now they weren't following through. They were abandoning me, just like my family.

I began to unravel a little more. They were just like the predator. I could feel myself growing very irritated. A storm was brewing inside me, and it was something like I had never, ever felt before, RAGE! So, I called the Sheriff's Department right after. They turned down my request as well.

I was now overcome with disappointment and despair. I mean, these were the people that I was turning to for help, the LAW, and they were not there for me, either.

I think mentally I believed that I was now WORTHLESS, and that their denial was a validation of that belief.

To me, at that time, being told to wait meant NEVER! My unstable mental state had caused me to become fixated on retrieving my belongings.

MY MIND KEPT racing back and forth, going in Post Traumatic Technicolor, reliving the sexual assaults and verbal abuse, over and over again. And now, this asshole had all my things, too. It was all too much for me to take.

I called all the people that were supposed to help me move. Much to my horror, some of them even complimented the predator on how cooperative he was when they called to cancel out on the seizing of my property.

"How could they say that he was CO-OPERATIVE, or anything good about him? I knew another color of the predator, black, the color of death. I simply cringed! But how could they know, it wasn't their fault, I hadn't shared all the torture I had been through.

I ate and ate. I threw up again and again. I was so hot, I was so exhausted and unwell. The blackness was taking over. I collapsed on the bed and sleep until the next day.

ON JUNE THIRTEENTH I was in and out of consciousness, the withdrawal effect from not being drugged by the predator, I believe, had kicked in. I was almost dead on the inside. I should have been hospitalized, but Lynn didn't recognize the symptoms of crash and burn. Besides, she was busy working at a new driving position at Coke, that she had just started, and she herself was overcome with exhaustion from the labor and the stifling heat and humidity of the weather.

Post Traumatic symptoms and rage were now consuming me. I felt it come over me that afternoon like a tidal wave, from the top of my head to the tips of my toes. It was fight or flight now.

As a last resort, in an attempt to be saved, I somehow pulled up from my soul a speck of hope. I called up Dr. K.

I called his office, but he wasn't available. I left a frantic message on his answering machine for him to please call me. That I desperately needed to see him!

He never returned my call.

I HAD LIVED my life being a good little girl, following all the rules, constantly trying to please everyone all the time, all in the name of love. Often times even compromising on what I truly valued and believed, just to get along, and this had brought me to this place. All alone, in a room, with all that I had in four bags on the floor!

It reminded me of when we had collected my mom's belongings. All her things put in garbage bags, placed on the floor in the basement of my dad's house.

Then, like I had been smashed over the head with a bat, it struck me. I had become my mother, a woman with no place to go, who nobody wanted, her clothes and things on the FLOOR.

It was late afternoon when I crossed over to the other side. I had asked, no, begged for help from my family, the police, the Sheriff's Department, and now Dr. K. All figures of authority, and not one of them was there for me.

I began to panic now. If they couldn't help me with getting my belongings back, how could they protect me from the predator? I wasn't afraid of him killing me, I was crumbling at the thought of him taking me and continuing the sexual torture.

Why, he might even do this to other women or young girls. He probably had. The predator must be stopped!

The heat was consuming, and my body and mind were spinning wildly, I was broken. I was once only suicidal, now an evangelist on a crusade to rid the world of myself *and* the demonic predator.

MARTIN LUTHER KING said "Violence is a result of hopelessness and despair." All my resources, in my mind, were dried up. I was way beyond hopelessness, I was desperate. Desperate to right all that had ever been wronged.

I drove myself to the bank and withdrew 500.00 in cash. I then headed to Riley's Gun Shop in Hooksett, NH. I felt nothing at this point, I had become numb. I was on a mission.

I had never been in a gun shop in my entire life. There was something empowering about it, to be able to control life and death. I went to the counter. There was a young salesclerk there. I told him that I needed a gun to protect myself. He showed me a small gun that fit in my hand. I held it in my right hand, my left hand passing over its form. The hopelessness that I had felt dissolved in an instant. I was in charge now.

"Have you ever shot a gun before?" The young clerk asked me. "There is a shooting range on Brown Ave. in Manchester, and you might want to go there and practice. It will help you know how to handle the weapon."

"Oh thank you, I will," I told the clerk.

As I held the gun in my hand, I felt like a superhero. I was unstoppable, invincible!

"I'll take it," I told the clerk.

"I'll need your driver's license. I've got to do a background check."

I reached into my purse, pulled out my wallet, opened it and removed my license. I handed it to the clerk.

"Thank you," he said. "It will be a couple of minutes to process this."

"All right," I replied.

The bullets of consciousness could not penetrate my fight back vest. I had fallen into a deep dark hole.

I became anxious as I waited for the clerk to do the background check. Would I be denied the purchase of the gun because of the restraining order? Had I come this far only to be turned away? I began to pace back and forth down the aisles in the store, pretending to check out the merchandise.

"You are all set," the store clerk called out. "Would you like some bullets with your handgun?"

"Yes," I answered, relieved that the gun was going to be mine, all mine.

I took my purchase and headed to my truck. I would return to Lynn's. I planned to conceal the weapon in my bedroom.

That was it. Problems solved!

Tomorrow it would be all over with.

TWENTY

THE CLAWS OF heat and humidity were embedded in me the night of June 13, 2001. I tried to relax in a pool of my own sweat. Weather like that only fueled my fighter instinct. Besides, I was on my third night without sleep, and I had hardly any food in my frail body.

I woke up at about two or three in the morning.

I needed to get up before anyone in the apartment. Lynn had no idea about the gun hidden in my room, nor the plan I had to take my life.

I quietly rose, took out some paper and envelopes. I also removed the gun from the case it came in. I had concealed it under my bed. I held the small handgun in my hands for a moment.

I wasn't afraid of the predator anymore. I felt safe and powerful. I then put the gun into my pocketbook and continued on with my suicide plot.

I wanted to make sure that those that I cared deeply about would know how I felt about them, and share some of the money I had left. My daughters were already in my will, but my closest friends were not.

I wrote my farewell notes to Judy, Karen, Lynn and some others. I vaguely remember crying so hard as I wrote that my vision was blurred. I could barely see. I will miss you all so much.

"I love you all," I said to myself as I wrote, using my hand to wipe away tears of despair.

I believe I wrote notes to my daughters Kristen and Sarah. I cried even harder. "I love you both so much. You were my whole life. I was so proud to be your mom. I am so sorry that I wasn't a good mother. I will go so that you won't have to come visit me like I had to visit my mother in an institution."

I truly believed that I would end up just like her, and I wouldn't do that to my children. Ending my life was much better.

As I finished writing the letters to my daughters, something came over me. I saw the bags of clothes on the floor.

"Oh my god, NO," and a shocking realization ran through my veins. The predator was right, I had become just like my mother.

I placed stamps on all the letters. It was like I was there, but I wasn't, like I was watching myself on television. I then gathered up the letters and put them in a small plastic grocery bag.

I slid my right hand into my pocketbook toward the concealed weapon and pulled it out. It was still there. I reached down into the other bag that had the bullets in it and placed them inside my pocketbook also, along with my wallet, a notebook and a pen.

The silence in the apartment was uncomfortable, and I was so afraid that Lynn or her boyfriend would wake up. Then everything would be spoiled. Seeing them or talking to them would shift my focus, and I didn't want that to happen. I know that the strength that I had mustered up to take this action could disappear at any moment.

"Just take the bags and go quickly and quietly," I told myself. "GO!"

So, in one swift sweeping motion with my left hand the bags were gathered. The right hand free to grab the set of keys on the dresser, and I was off into the darkest hour, that hour that comes just before dawn.

I was a dead woman tiptoeing, walking and driving to end this journey.

IT WAS ABOUT 4:45 am, June 14, 2001. I was driving on the back roads in Goffstown, NH. The bullets and the gun ready. This was it. There would be no more tears to cry. NO more feelings to feel. Nothing at all!

The thought of leaving this earth was so appealing now. I began to feel relieved that justice would be served. Death for Kathleen Ann Rioux and the predator would make the world a better place. There would be peace.

No one could hurt me anymore. I couldn't hurt anyone and the predator couldn't either.

HE WAS STANDING in front of the door as I came toward him. He was heading out, keys in his right hand locking the dead bolt to the main entrance, a bag in the other hand.

He looked to his left, over his shoulder, to see who it was. Recognizing me immediately he said, "You back for more, bitch?" And then he laughed at me.

I stopped in my tracks the minute I heard the haunting sound of his voice.

"I can't believe you went to the police! I was done with your sorry ass anyway!" His words were like vomit spewing from his lips, as if he had already rehearsed what he would say to me at our next encounter.

I was filled with both fear and even more rage now. This animal had to be put out of his misery once and for all, no logic, just fight back.

I reached into my purse and placed my right hand over the small revolver and pulled it out so it was in view. Then, I slowly raised the loaded gun, the bullets put in just minutes ago in the car. The only emotion now was the rage. Like a cornered cat that had been beaten down to a pulp, it was time, time to fight back!

"Oh look at you," the predator said laughing at me once again. "You don't have the guts to shoot that gun at me." Then he started to come towards me.

I couldn't speak, or even yell. I tried to tell him to stay away from me or I'd shoot, but no sound came from my mouth, the adrenaline had frozen my vocal chords.

Oh my god! Oh my god!

He's going to get me. He's going to rape me again, and again like he did before, I thought, trembling out of control.

Then, I closed my eyes and began to shoot the gun at the predator. It was my divine animal right to protect myself from this demon!

As the shots rang out the sound was deafening, and the gun kicked back almost knocking me down. When the bullets were used up the gun clicked. Trying to comprehend what had just occurred, I opened my eyes to see why the predator hadn't reached me.

He was lying on the ground. He was in a fetal position, struck by a ricocheting bullet. I felt nothing for him, or the situation. I was emotionally vacant. I just looked into his demonic eyes, turned my back to him and in slow motion returned to my vehicle, which was parked outside the building on St. Anselm's Drive.

Still controlled by adrenaline, the fight response became flight, and I walked to my vehicle like I was in an out of body experience, in slow motion. I fumbled to retrieve my keys, my hands trembling out of control as I tried to put the key in to the ignition. Finally the truck started, and I headed north to finish the business for the day, my demise.

Still shell-shocked, I had cut myself off from the rest of the world. I somehow drove myself up to the base of Mt. Washington, the first mountain I had ever climbed, the last place I would ever see. Now I became focused on committing suicide.

I ENDED UP in the parking lot to the left of the toll booth. When I arrived, the booth was unattended. It was just before the regular business hour, early A.M. I was relieved that no one was around at that time. I could now continue with the final chapter of this nightmare.

I gazed up towards the trail head and nostalgically recalled that this was an amazing first climb for me. I thought with my warped mind about killing myself at the very top, but I was too tired and weak to attempt it!

I began to weep bitterly, flooded with different emotions, now thinking about the day's events and of my life overall. It was all so very bittersweet.

The greatest joy of life for me was to be a mother. It was! I had a chance to do that, to give unconditional love and receive it, and nothing else really mattered.

I was tired, so tired. And as beams of light began to stream through the forest, I fell into a deep sleep inside my truck. I slept for a while, waking to the sounds of the park coming to life with the staff, then the visitors. They were setting up for the Mt. Washington Road Race.

I would have to wait now, suicide on hold, as I did not want to draw any attention to myself.

It was getting really hot in my vehicle. So I decided to get out and sit by the babbling brook that was right by the parking area. I took the bottle of water that I had and headed towards a shaded spot. Once I found it, I lay down on the grass, and passed out again.

I was again awoken by the sounds of the staff and others. I got up and walked back to the truck. I sat in the truck, turned it on so that I could listen to some music.

I took the notebook that I had brought with me to write my last words in. I was reflective and to the point, being as positive as I could, under the circumstances. My message was one of being grateful for all the beautiful moments I had experienced. You think that would have jolted me into reality to stop this madness, but it did not.

There was, in my mind, nothing left to live for anymore.

I WAITED UNTIL darkness fell, believing that the lack of light would allow me to complete my deed. Also, hopefully there would be a lack of spectators to see or hear anything tonight. I was so afraid that someone would try to interfere with my plans.

I moved my truck from the parking area at the base of Mt. Washington down the road to the left, pulling it over on the wide shoulder of the road.

A small glimmer of consciousness was surprised that I had remained at the base of the mountain all day without anyone approaching me, or calling the authorities. Perhaps that was because my death was supposed to happen, my clouded mind decided.

"Just count to three, then pull the trigger," I coached myself. "Put the gun inside your mouth. Push it up into your mouth until you touch the roof of your mouth with the gun. That way you will die instantly."

I was now disconnecting almost totally, the little light that was left in me, slowly fading out.

"Count to three. One…Two…Three…and it will be all over."

I placed the gun inside my mouth. I pushed the gun way up inside until it touched the roof of my mouth. Then, I counted: One, Two, Three.

I couldn't do it! I tried again.

I put the gun inside my mouth. I pushed the gun up until it touched the roof of my mouth once again. Then I counted.

"One…Two…Three…"

As I was about to pull the trigger, I believe I was struck with divine intervention. I thought about my two daughters, Kristen and Sarah.

"My Kristen, and my Sarah."

I couldn't do this to them. I couldn't! I would be doing the same thing that my mother had done to me, left me behind. I was not Dolores. I was Kathleen Rioux. I loved them too much to leave them this way.

I broke down and cried and cried, consciousness melting over my distorted thoughts, taking over.

I almost took my life over what was said and done to me. I would face whatever I had to face now. I would do it in the name of love of Kristen, Sarah and myself.

TWENTY-ONE

SHORTLY AFTERWARDS, I turned myself into the Conway Police Department. I parked my truck outside the station. I walked inside and spoke to the officer at the window. "I shot my gun at someone today. I am not sure how severe a condition he is in. My name is Kathleen."

He instructed me to follow him into a room off the waiting area. He closed the door behind me and it locked shut, I wasn't going anywhere now. He told me to sit down and wait. I followed his directions.

The officer was gone briefly; I assumed that he was checking out my story.

When he returned, he told me that there was a warrant out for my arrest. I needed to remove my shoes, and give him the keys to my vehicle and my purse. He told me that they would be searching the inside of my truck.

I was patted down to see if I had any other weapons on my person. Then I was led to a cell, and told that the Goffstown Police Department would be coming to get me in the morning. I went in. I asked if I could have some water to drink.

"Yes," the officer said. "I'll be back in a while."

After what seemed like hours, he returned with a small cup of water. He handed it to me and waited while I drank it down so he could have the cup back. I handed it back to him, and he took it, expressionless.

I tried to explain myself. I was sobering up from the post traumatic binge I had been on, reality creeping in like the early morning fog. But he was uninterested in my story and simply replied, "You should get some rest now."

Still in shock, I cooperated.

I was caged, but oddly, I felt safe from the world outside.

THE GOFFSTOWN POLICE sent a male and female officer to come and get me. Retrieved like a lost dog. They offered me some water to drink. I drank it down, I was so thirsty; I hadn't had anything since the night before.

I was considered a flight risk, so I was handcuffed and shackled, a chain connecting my hands and feet. I was then led to the cruiser outside, the female officer guiding me, as I could hardly walk with the chain binding my feet.

Once we arrived at the Goffstown Police station I was brought in the back way. The handcuffs and shackles were removed. Then my fingerprints were taken by a female officer, holding each finger to the ink pad to take the prints. She was nice enough, just doing her job. The chemicals in my system were wearing off now and I wanted to try to defend my actions to her, help her to understand my plight.

My mind was still cluttered, confused. I wanted to share the details, but I could not find the words.

I was read my rights and charged with attempted murder. One of the detectives approached me and wanted me to tell him what had happened, but something inside me told me to hold my tongue and I said I would wait until I spoke to an attorney. He reminded me of a vulture waiting to pick away at the remains of roadkill.

As the words left the officer's mouth, the terrible, horrible truth of the situation rocked my body. I would be held accountable for my actions.

I remember making a request for an apple. I usually started my day off with one, and in some way I needed it to bring some sense of normalcy to this madness. Like, if I could take a bite of a juicy apple, chew it slowly, taste it, and hear the snap of the skin when your teeth break into it, everything would be all right.

My wish was granted, and somehow, some way, I would make it.

THE FINGERPRINTING WAS nothing compared to what was about to occur next. I heard the footsteps coming toward the cell door.

The clinking sound of metal chains caught my attention. The key to unlock the door was placed in the lock and the heavy metal door swung open.

There in the doorway of the cell stood two officers, the same male and female who had transported me from Conway to Goffstown.

"We'll be taking you to the Valley Street Jail, in Manchester. You will have to be shackled and handcuffed again for the ride there." The male officer spoke like he was talking to the wall.

The shocked haze was still there for me, thank God, as they told me to spread my legs so that the female officer could shackle my ankles.

"Put your hands behind your back," she instructed me, "so I can handcuff you." Once again, I could not allow myself to feel anything.

I numbed myself for my own preservation, my survival, a skill that I had mastered so well over the years. I never thought that skill would come in so handy!

I was then brought down a long hallway where another huge metal dungeon-like door was unlocked. I was led out into the morning light towards the police car parked a few feet from the exit.

The drive to the jail was short. I was so glad, because my wrists were in excruciating pain from the handcuffs. The door was opened for me, my head pushed on for clearance and I was led into jail!

I was led into the booking room. It was a large room with a counter to my left. As I passed through another large metal door, the sound of the loud clunk as it closed shut was another reminder of where I was.

There were three men dressed in brown uniforms; all of them had short military style haircuts. Expressionless Correctional Officers, who would be checking me into this place, and with a commanding voice, almost a yell, one said, "Your name."

Still in a frozen state I said, "Kathleen Rioux."

"Address."

I became nervous, my voice cracked and lowered as I answered him. He couldn't hear me so he hollered back, "Louder."

I repeated my address in a louder tone, and I was now trembling.

I wanted this to be over with and no more attention to be drawn to me.

This time, I was loud enough, and he entered the information I gave into his computer. As he did this, I was able to look behind me.

There, to my horror, was a room filled with men of all different shapes, sizes and from all walks of life, behind a large glass window.

Like spectacles in a freak show, the glass separated us, and I was appalled to see humans and not animals sitting, standing and staring. Some men looked so sick, that not to hospitalize them was criminal!

I had never been in trouble like this before. I had never seen anything like the Valley Street Jail before.

As I glanced around at my new surroundings, still handcuffed and shackled, I waited at attention for my next direction. Even my breath was in sync, for fear I would be severely reprimanded.

Another one of the officers came from behind the counter and then towards me. He removed the shackles from around my ankles and said, "I'm going to remove your handcuffs now. Don't make any sudden moves or I'll knock you down to the floor so hard you won't know what hit you."

I stood like a statue, frightened to death. My stomach began to turn violently now, and I felt like vomiting, but I talked myself out of it.

"Just do what he asks," I told myself. "Just do what he asks and everything will be all right." Everything will be all right?

"Take off your sneakers," was my next order, "and put them over there with the others." I quickly obliged and placed them next to the growing collection of footwear by the wall where the large glass window divider was, where all the incarcerated men were.

He pulled his large key ring from its attachment on the right side of his belt, and thumbed through the bunch of keys until he found the one he wanted. The key was then placed into his right hand as he headed toward another large metal door with a small window about eight inches by eight inches, the thick glass in the opening intertwined with wire.

As he opened the door the sounds of people seeped out, female voices, two maybe three.

"Get in here and wait until your name is called."

I went forward toward the opened door, did what I was told, anxious and petrified as to what would come. I came to the opening and peered in. There, to my astonishment and disgust was a seven by thirteen room. It had a filthy gray cement floor, red concrete blocks for the walls and a metal seven by three foot bench, complete with a pad about an inch in thickness for comfort.

The first thing that caught my eye were the pint sized milk cartons and Styrofoam plates—with what looked like left over bologna sandwiches—strewn about on the floor.

My nose validated my vision of the milk and the bologna as I went further into this cage. I felt even more nauseated now as the metal door was slammed shut behind me.

The cell had three other women in it. One woman had blonde hair, partially pulled up with a barrette holding back her bangs, probably in her mid- forties. She was dressed in loosely fitted jeans and a pale yellow short-sleeve shirt, and shoeless. She was one of the women sitting on the bench. She smiled as I entered, and I was taken aback to see someone like her here.

The other woman sitting beside her was much younger—eighteen, maybe nineteen. She was scantily dressed in a halter top, with short shorts. Her brown hair just reached her shoulders. She was very thin, and talked non-stop. She just kept up the conversation she was having with the blonde-haired lady, never even looking up to acknowledge my presence.

The third woman was leaning up against the cell wall. She looked very distraught, a comb hadn't touched her hair in days, nor had she bathed; body odor caught my nostrils from the slight breeze she created as she paced back and forth. She scared me, and I felt that if I said the wrong thing, she would explode. Her eyes were a warning to stay away, as well as the conversation she was having with herself.

Reluctantly, I asked the blonde, forty-something woman to push over so that I could sit down.

"This has been a long day. Could you please push over so I can sit down," I asked politely, not really knowing if she too was a time bomb ready to go off.

"Sure," she replied in a friendly manner.

She put her hand out and introduced herself. "Hi, my name is Shirley. What's yours?"

Shocked at her normalcy I said, "Hi, I'm Kathleen."

Shirley and I chatted. We shared our tales of woe, and how we ended up here. The young eighteen-year-old joined in too. Her name was Josie. The distraught women would comment every now and then, most of what she said made no sense. We listened anyway though, for who were any of us to know what was sensible and what wasn't? Her name was Margaret.

All of a sudden, like being struck by a bolt of lightning, it dawned on me how much we were all similar. I felt a sense of relief, as I didn't feel so odd, so alone. We all had one common thread: we were where we were because we didn't feel we had any value. None of us had ever felt valuable!

My heart went out to Margaret. When she was arrested, she was hauled off in only a nightgown! No undergarments, just this flimsy transparent knee high thing. To do such a thing to a human being seemed like such a rape of her dignity. Luckily, she was too confused to know most of what was going on.

SIX HOURS passed before I was called to come out. Two hours before, I had asked to go to the bathroom. I had to shout it out through a small five-inch square opening in the thick metal door that separated us from those in authority. Nobody paid any attention. Not one Correctional Officer even acknowledged my basic need. I was outraged. I could have gone in an empty milk carton like Josie did I guess, but I just couldn't bring myself to stoop that low.

The officer pounded on the door and called out my last name really loud.

"Rioux." It was a tough female voice. She opened the door and commanded, "Everyone else needs to stay away from the door."

I mean really! Where would you run to, even if you did get out? I stepped out following her instructions like a pet dog.

"Step up against this wall," she barked, and pointed to the left of the door. I did.

I was led down a small corridor. Once again, another metal door was before me. "Stand over there while I unlock the door." I did.

The door opened and I was told to go in first. Another counter stood before me, a smaller one than the counter I checked in at, sort of like a dry-cleaning counter. Another female correctional officer, dressed in her best browns, stood behind that counter.

"I have to go to the bathroom," I said desperately. "I've had to go for the last two hours."

My words did not even faze them. One of them said, "Okay you can go in here, but I have to go in with you." The words rolled off her tongue like it was nothing.

My hesitation and the look on my face elicited her comment of, "You going to go or what? We haven't got all day!"

It was all too much to understand. This was not the place to question anything, your rights as a human being were stripped from you when you checked in, and your dignity had to be left behind.

I was accompanied to a bathroom with no door. I just did what I had to do. I didn't think about anything, as she stood in the doorway watching me urinate. It was one of the most humiliating moments of my life, with many more yet to come, but I didn't know it.

"STEP OVER HERE," the female correctional officer behind the counter ordered, and as I did what I was told, and stepped forward, I noticed that there were many black garment bags behind the counter. When I was a few feet from the counter she told me to, "Stop right there."

"Here, take this bag and hang it on that hook to your right on the wall," the female said. So, I grabbed the bag that was practically thrown at me and placed it on the hook. "Unzip it," she barked. I did.

"Now, remove all your clothes and place them in the garment bag along with your sneakers. Then you'll be searched."

What? Oh my god, no! NO, NO, NO! I was blown away by this most disgusting and dehumanizing request. Were my ears deceiving me? I was frozen once again as I tried to process this, trying to keep my composure.

"Are you deaf? I said remove all your clothes and put them in that bag! After I strip search you, you are to take a shower. Make sure you get your hair wet too."

Just do it. Just do it. Do it fast! I talked to myself, going into shutdown mode to cope with this. Kind of like when you go for your pap test.

Shaking and quivering, I removed my clothes and put them into the death black garment bag, more like a body bag if you ask me, and I stood there naked and vulnerable in front of this correctional officer.

She had me raise my hands over my head and, like I was a slab of meat, she checked my body over. First was the front part: under my arms, my breast, inside my mouth, and the inside of my ears. It sickened me so much that I thought that I would throw up in her face.

Next was the back of my body. I was then asked to squat and cough, to make sure my rectum and vagina didn't contain any illegal substances.

When this horrific ritual was over, I breathed deeply, as I thought I might pass out. The shower came next. I stepped into a filthy gray single shower stall, closed the curtain, and turned on the shower.

The water was freezing cold, on purpose maybe, to add insult to injury. I mean, why was I thinking that the shower would be any different from the rest of this place? There was nothing comforting here.

I opened the shower curtain and the officer threw me a dingy hand towel and told me to dry myself off. I must have been too lackadaisical, and she screamed at me, "Hurry up, we don't have all day!"

Pressures of the work environment, I guess.

There was no time allowed for a discussion, and I dried my frail body all over as quickly as I could, anything to please this task master. This was not the treatment of someone innocent until proven guilty.

I was guilty to them already.

MY NEW ATTIRE was placed on the counter, and I was told to dress in the items placed before me. There was a dingy white sports bra, from 1980 maybe, and gray underpants. I wanted to refuse them and ask for new ones, but quickly dismissed the idea. Orange, burlap like, heavy cotton bottoms with an elastic waistband and a matching orange v- neck short-sleeve top made of the same material.

The officer then came from behind the counter and said, "Stand over there by the wall, spread your arms up over your head and put your hands up against the wall, spread your legs."

I followed her instructions without any hesitation, the zombie I had now become, had been forced to become. I couldn't let myself be touched by this. Now, as I write this, tears leave my eyes to validate the feelings I held in back then. I was handcuffed behind my back, and my legs were shackled again, and then I was led out of the garment room and back into the booking room. I was then told to wait on the bench up against the wall to my right, the chains clinking as I walked toward the bench.

"You'll be interviewed by our on-site social worker. Wait here until your name is called."

As I waited, and waiting seemed to be the agenda imposed upon you, like it or not, I looked and I listened. I saw the faces of men and women, young and old, short and tall, with varying degrees of life-styles. I heard their voices, some loud, some soft, some spiced up with profanity and some silent. We all, however, had one thing in common, we were all here because somewhere along the way our value had been compromised by those around us, and sadly we believed them.

The reality of all this just punched me in the gut.

I FELT NOTHING and said nothing. I just existed now as I went through one locked door after another. Not being able to go through the next set of doors without the set behind me being first secured. The security amazed me, and although I couldn't get out, the predator couldn't get in, and on some level, I felt safe.

There were four other women being inducted when I was. There was only one pod for women at the Valley Street Jail. The reality of where I was now hit me even harder, as the metal door swung open into a large room, kind of like a cafeteria with the round tables and chairs bolted to the floor. The cells surrounded this large room on two floors.

We were the abandoned, the lost, the confused, the women that were thrown away. And without even hearing their stories, I could see all the pain in their eyes as I stepped into the pod.

A male correctional officer was manning the pod and he approached us. We were unchained from one another, one by one, as the female officer stood beside each of us. She would order us to face the wall. This was the ritual of removing the handcuffs and shackles, and then both officers escorted you to your cell immediately.

"You will need to stay in here for now. Soon you will get to join the regular population."

Of course I had no idea of what he was telling me. Everything was vague. "Here for now," turned out to be FIVE DAYS with only TWO hours out for a shower and to make a phone call or two. I would have totally freaked out then had I known the truth! Sometimes, it's better not to know.

I was suicidal for the first few days. Being caged does that to you, and if it weren't for the help of Sister Margarite, a dear friend of a friend, who was a counselor at the jail, I would have never made it out sane.

I was informally introduced to her in my orange attire on day three when I was called from outside my cell door.

"Rioux, you have a visitor," said the male CO in through my cell window.

The fact that I could get out was the first joy, the second joy was that I could visit with someone, anyone, and I was let out and led to a room with windows. As I entered, I had no idea who she was, but it surely seemed like divine intervention! As the door closed behind me, she greeted me with a hug, and she held my hand, and continued to hold it while we talked about my predicament.

"It's okay," she said. "Be gentle with yourself. You've just bit off more than you could chew."

And with those words, and her gentle human touch, I knew I would make it!

And I did.

She was an angel sent to me, a treasured gift, a member of my newly formed family.

WELL, THAT'S HOW I got here. In the name of loving everyone else but the most important person, MYSELF! And fifty-five days later I was released on my own personal recognizance. Go figure, because at an earlier court appearance, my bail had been set for 100,000 dollars!

My weeks of pleading with my attorney, Gregory Swope, to get me out had come to fruition. It was court ordered that I would stay with my brother Jim and his family until a trial date was set.

I was in my cell when the CO came to tell me that I was going to be released. I was shaking with such disbelief I could barely say a word. I did manage a "Thank You."

"Gather your things together and another CO will be here to discharge you soon," the CO told me. I wanted to yell and scream out about my release, but I didn't. Inside though, I was hooting and hollering.

Then all of sudden the CO who had told me of my great news then said, "I'm sorry, I was only kidding. You've got to stay here." She said it to me laughing then turned and walked away.

I was simply dumbfounded. Did I just hear what she said?

Then she came back into the cell, as I sat on my bunk not knowing what to think. Then in a loud condescending tone she calmly tells me that she was just kidding.

I guess the expression on my face from her cruel joke was enough to elicit laughter from all the women in the pod. I guess she needed to feel powerful, at my expense.

I didn't care though. I simply waited patiently for my escort to come. Finally, after what seemed like forever, a female CO came to retrieve me. I was cuffed and shackled once again and brought down to the booking room. I should have complained about the accommodations and the service, but I remained silent! Then I entered the room where I had my very first strip search, my VERY last for sure!

I dressed myself quickly for fear they would change their minds and keep me here longer. When I dressed, I left the room and went before the desk where I had been stripped of all my personal belongings: my rings, earrings and hair clip, which were carelessly thrown into a brown paper bag and handed to me.

I had to sign a waiver to verify that all my things were returned to me. I did, not even caring if everything was there or not.

"You can't leave until the bailiff arrives. You need to sign a contract with him."

"All right," I complied. "Thank you." I sat down on the bench that the CO had pointed to.

Soon after, the bailiff came through the large glass security doors. He was polished, and all about business, cold and calculated—occupational hazard I guess— and I picked up on the cue from his body language that I should refrain from any small talk, and just sign the "damn" papers so that he could leave.

"You better follow all the rules that you just signed for, or your sweet little ass will be back here faster than the speed of light. Understand?"

"Yes," I responded.

The bailiff gave me a copy of the agreement and left as abruptly as he had come.

One of the CO's at the desk looked up at me, "Do you want to call someone to come and pick you up?"

"Yes," I answered.

"Use the pay phone over there." He pointed to the phone attached to the wall to my right. I walked over to the pay phone. My gate a little unsteady, and I began to shake a little. I couldn't become unglued just yet. *Just be strong and make the phone call*, I told myself.

"HELLO. HI. YES, it's me Kathleen. Please come and get me!" I said as calmly as I could. I didn't want to reveal the quivering that my body was doing in my speech.

"All right," the voice on the other end of the phone said.

"I'll be waiting outside," I told my brother. And the Thunder Moon waxed, just a little.

TWENTY-TWO

I HAD CHOSEN attorney Gregory Swope to represent me. He was one of three lawyers that my brother Jim had arranged for me to meet. Affordability was the deciding factor. I had about $30,000.00 dollars left in my account after my divorce, and ironically, that was Mr. Swope's fee for his services. The other attorneys' fees were $50,000.00 dollars and up!

I was in jail at the time of attorney selection. I didn't qualify for public defender because of my LARGE, yah right, bank account. So, the pressure was on to get legal representation as soon as possible.

Before Mr. Swope would take my case, I needed to sign over the whole amount. The whole $30,000.00, for better or worse, win or lose! So the account was emptied, after all the paper work giving him permission. Now, I was not only incarcerated, but I was penniless as well!

GREGORY SWOPE WAS middle-aged, cocky and arrogant. I believe though, that those were the very qualities necessary in winning this case for me. He wasn't thorough enough was my gut feeling. I was worried that he would not serve me well. My fate was in his hands, and he seemed detached.

I needed to prove why I did what I did. What one individual, the predator, had driven me to do. Every time I went to meet with Mr. Swope I repeated my story, my plight. Something had to be done to give my case solid ground for my behavior.

Finally, when it was close to the trial, he arranged for me to meet with Dr. Brown. She was a psychiatrist that practiced in Boston. She had agreed to meet with me to give me a diagnosis to present to the state.

I drove myself to Boston to meet with her. She was to the point and all business, but I wasn't there to make a friend, I needed her to write up a report to prove my innocence.

Our first meeting lasted a few hours. It was a trip back into my past. We discussed my earliest recollection up until just before the incident. That first meeting was utterly exhausting. I had to sit in my car for about an hour just to compose myself so I could drive back to Manchester.

The second and last meeting took place in an attorney's office. He was an acquaintance of Mr. Swope and had allowed us to meet there as to make the drive for both of us easier.

Dr. Brown was again direct with her questioning. It sometimes even felt more like an interrogation, but I felt she was justified, for I believe she was seeking the truth for my diagnosis, and for some reason I trusted her.

Her conclusion of was that I was suffering from Post Traumatic Stress Syndrome. It was a combination of some of the events prior to my relationship with the predator. However, it was what he had done to me that caused the severe breakdown of my mental state.

SOMETHING INSIDE ME now whispered that everything would be all right after my meetings with Dr. Brown. I just needed to believe, and in the name of love of Kathleen, I did! Attorney Swope prepared me for the worst-case scenario at the last few visits I had with him before the trial, at his office in Concord.

"Kathy, this is an attempted murder case. A self-defense verdict is not likely. You need to prepare for a sentencing of anywhere between 7 – 15 years minimum!

"Believe me," he continued, "I know what the bastard did to you. I'm working hard to collect all the evidence necessary to free you. I've got some convincing testimonies from your counselor and the eating disorder center, and Dr. Brown's report is certainly instrumental in your defense."

Mr. Swope had told me that there was trouble with having a trial. He said that if there were some women on the jury, believe it or not, they might hate me for what I did. He further explained that some of them were in similar situations and had thought about doing the same thing I did. To fight back to their abusive husbands, boyfriends, and even their fathers, but they didn't have the courage! They didn't have the strength.

"Not you though, Kathy, you did it. You stood up to the son of a bitch, the predator, and they are jealous of you."

"Jealous! Are you kidding me?"

"NO! They hate you because you ended the abuse."

Well, I must have sat there for a long time, tears running down my cheeks. They would hate me for defending myself against a monster. It seemed inconceivable, all too much to take, as my mind began to spin. Mr. Swope said that the meeting was over, and I said, "Thanks," as I headed out of the room to my truck parked outside.

Swope's words, You are probably going to jail. You are probably going to jail, were repeating over and over again, stinging and burning my brain.

Was he kidding? He knew what the animal had done to me. *He knew!* I said to myself. And after each doomsday meeting, I would let the poisonous words spew from his lips, and I would hold my tongue. He really didn't allow me to comment or discuss anything, it was a lecture, not a conversation, but he was working for me.

Then I would leave and get into my vehicle, take a long deep breathe to let all his fear wash off me, and then I would think of myself as free, and tell myself, "No Mr. Gregory Swope, I don't think so!"

The fear of those around me and my attorney's lack of faith was very strong. I was presented with an opportunity to plea bargain. I would plead guilty to the charges, with the hope that my sentencing would be lighter. Once I signed the plea bargain, I would forfeit my rights to a trial, my ability to vote and other penalties.

I agonized with this proposition. I felt so strongly about saying what I needed to say, I wanted my innocence to be proven. Now, looking back, it was really about the money. A trial costs money, lots of it, and my well had run dry. I wasn't rich, so my fate was sealed, I believe.

I ended up taking the plea bargain. And it wasn't a bargain at all! I was innocent!

The state had gathered all their evidence for my conviction. The case, however, seemed to have many unanswered questions. There were no past episodes of violence from me, and I was a woman who was an upstanding citizen. It seemed as though the turmoil had begun once I had become seriously involved with the predator.

The predator, however, had been injured as a result of the firearm that belonged to me. A bullet had bounced off the wall striking him, and the state would press hard on the seriousness of my actions.

TWENTY-THREE

THE SUN HAD already risen. The sun did not wake me on this Wednesday, July 24, 2002. It was the sound of my alarm clock, "Bonk, bonk, bonk.".

I had called this my bedroom for almost a year now. The room was located on the west side of a white colonial in the town of Hooksett, NH that belonged to my brother and his wife. It was a computer room before I came. It had been court ordered that I stay here, much better than jail.

Ironically, I had asked to come here to live when I had no place to go. When I was involved with the predator! I had been turned down though, because, "I had gotten myself into this mess, and I needed to get myself out." Something like that. I understand their decision now.

This was the day. A day unlike any other I had ever begun in my whole life. In fact, by the end of this day, my fate would be known. Known to my daughters, my family and friends, and yes, even to the community!

Unfortunately, I had become newsworthy. "There will be media coverage, the local television station will be covering this story, so be prepared," my attorney stated, without any emotion, as I left his office a month ago.

The hellish dark past of my childhood, adolescence and adulthood had finally caught up to me, had slammed me to the ground. I was trapped, pinned down and suffocating from the trauma. Nearly dead, I could not take the weight of anything anymore!

Everyone thought it was just one thing, but for me, it was years of raw sewage rotting out my soul. Not allowing me to be present, or to move forward. How can you, if you haven't tossed the past? The heavy baggage of physical abuse, verbal abuse, emotional abuse, brain washing, guilt, shame, rape and abandonment holding me down like iron chains. Like Dorothy, not knowing that I had the power to create a better reality for myself. Dorothy with her ruby slippers, me with being present. Tossing the past! Home is in your soul. It's you, being you.

I HAD SELECTED a green sleeveless rayon dress with small purple flowers for my court appearance. It was actually the same dress I had worn for a very important, happy celebration a few years ago. Mind blowing now, to think it would be worn for an occasion such as this.

My attorney had advised me to wear something nice. "You know, to make a good impression." Really, I thought to myself. Like I had to make myself look good. I had tried to make a good impression all my life and here is where I ended up.

So, after I showered, I put on the rayon dress. I would wear a cream color summer sweater over it when I reached the courtroom. I wasn't sure what the temperature would be like inside. It was July after all, and the air conditioning would be on. I didn't want to be shivering on the outside, like I felt a little, on the inside. Also, I didn't want to be anyone but MYSELF either.

I heard the stirring inside the dwelling, downstairs, in the kitchen. My brother, his wife and their son were all preparing for this day, too. And although there were no voices, the sound of their thoughts was deafening.

I didn't want to talk to them. In fact, the conversations while living with them were minimal. They were living in fear. It wasn't their fault, my brother and his wife, they didn't know any better. Besides my green floral dress, I was wearing my fear proof vest, and I didn't want it to get melted!

I headed down to the kitchen. I Prepared my usual breakfast of cereal, almond butter, and some sliced apples. I ate slowly, savoring every bite. I wanted to make sure that the meal would settle right on my stomach. My thoughts were focused, "The truth will set you free," and "Everything will be all right, everything will be all right," ran through my head, over and over. I finished eating and went back upstairs to finish getting ready.

Within a few minutes I was all properly groomed on the outside. I grabbed my purse, the keys to my pick-up truck, my sweater and proceeded down the stairs to the kitchen once again.

On the outside I was calm and centered.

"We'll be ready to leave in a few minutes," my brother said to me as I entered the kitchen area.

"No thank you. I'll drive myself."

"But what about your truck?" my brother called out after me.

"What about it?" I said over my shoulder, without any hesitation. I closed the door behind me, keeping my composure on the inside and out.

I had listened to the weatherman's forecast the night before on the radio in my upstairs bedroom, so I could dress accordingly. He was predicting a hot day, with temps of 80 degrees or more. He also said that there was going to be a full moon, the Thunder Moon.

I already knew about the Thunder Moon. It was on my Susan Branch calendar, a beautiful work of art, as well as informative, great for the heart and the soul.

"Yes everyone, there will be a full moon tonight. It is named the Thunder Moon," he said, "named by the Indians."

I went to my calendar and ran my fingers over the date. I felt the power of the Thunder Moon at that very moment. A good omen, and I believed that a great blessing would be bestowed upon me.

I never told anyone about the Thunder Moon.

I drove myself to the courthouse on that hot, steamy July morning because it was the action that I took for the belief in myself. The knowing that everything would be all right! That I was innocent of the charge of attempted murder. That I had acted in self-defense.

I felt that my brother and his wife, my attorney and others did not believe that I would be set free, their doubts and fears reeked, but my FEAR shield did not allow the stench to penetrate.

All their words and actions never got through to my light

throughout the last year or so. I refused to allow my light to be dowsed out by anyone's disbelief. I believed, and that was all that mattered.

I OPENED THE door to my Chevy S-10. The heat inside the cab hit my face as if I had opened the door to a pre-heated oven. I slid into the driver's side, closed the door and immediately opened the windows on the driver's side. I then reached over to open the window on the passenger's side of the cab. No Ac in this ride, unfortunately.

I backed into the street, and headed north. I reached for the radio button, pushed on it and music spilled out into the cab of the truck; I desperately needed a distraction. My destination was the Hillsborough County courthouse on Chestnut St., in Manchester, NH.

I got onto Bridge St. and headed west towards the city. Once I reached Chestnut St. I turned left and drove down the street until I came upon the courthouse, which was on the right. For a split second I thought about not stopping. To keep on driving to anywhere, any place other than here, but I didn't, no point, the consequences would be worse. Instead, I took the next right and parked at one of the open spots.

The parking spot had a meter, and I fed the machine as many quarters as I had. I wasn't sure how long the court hearing would last.

I took in three deep breaths with my eyes closed. I was ready to face the music of the courtroom now. Well, noise, if you will.

I opened the large glass door and went through. Then I went through another set. There were a few security guards waiting to check you and your belongings out. I handed them my purse, which would be put on a conveyer belt and x-rayed. I walked through the metal detector. I thought to myself as I made it through without setting off the alarm, "Unarmed, but still dangerous."

As I looked up, I noticed my attorney on the other side of the detector. He was standing by one of the benches.

"Hi," he said. "We'll head upstairs and go over what will be going on during the hearing."

I really didn't feel that my attorney had done everything in his power to defend me. As a matter of fact, I felt a little betrayed. The plea bargain that I had felt I had been forced into, by putting fear into me, a novice in the criminal justice system at the time, seemed like an easy, cruel cop out on his part.

At one point he had said, "Prison is so much better than jail. There is a lot more to do there."

"Imagine that," I thought to myself as his words smashed into my ear drums. "Then you can go there for me."

This was not the time, however, for anger, resentment or regrets. It was a time to rise to the occasion with integrity and wisdom!

In the last year, due to my law-breaking ordeal, I had truly realized how unjust the justice system was. How a person could be hand-cuffed, shackled, strip searched, and kept in a cell for five days with only two hours out a day and incarcerated for 55 days without even being found guilty!

REALLY!

My attorney was rambling on about something, the plan. I did not let anything he said sink in, all his words and actions. I simply nodded, and responded, "Yes, all right, all right."

In my mind I was saying over and over a chant taught to me by a woman I had met while working at R&D Cleaners in Hooksett as a dry cleaning counter clerk. You never know who will bring you the tools you need to flourish. You just need to pay very close attention.

Anyway, one day she came into the shop while I was working. My fear shield had been pelted with fear from those that I had to live with, my attorney and others. The pressures of the upcoming trial, my ex-husband wanting an annulment, and the workload were all too much! As she placed down her dry-cleaning order on the counter, well, everything just hit me, and I broke down and began to cry.

She came behind the counter and embraced me. I mean here is this perfect stranger comforting me. I didn't give her any of the specifics, but told her that I was facing a horrible situation and wasn't sure about the outcome.

"What do you want?" she asked me.

I looked at her, completely stunned.

"What?" I looked into her eyes, drying mine with the tissue she had gently placed into my right hand.

"Don't tell me. Just write down what you want. It might even be a list of what you want. Read the list three times a day. Then chant these four words after each time you read the list. "Nam, Myaho (me-ya-ho), Renge, Kyo." She chanted them as she said each word.

She repeated the four words once again, chanting them as she said them.

"Nam...Myaho...Renge...Kyo," she chanted.

It sounded a bit ridiculous at first, but for some reason I believed that it would work. I reached for a piece of paper and wrote the words she had said.

"You will get what you ask for?"

God knows I had always used prayer to get through all the dysfunction of my childhood, adolescence and into adulthood. However, the events after I filed for divorce, from about 1998 up until 2001, primarily the rape, left me asking God why, but you can never really ask why, can you, and I stopped praying. I believed I was a victim.

SO HERE I WAS in the courthouse, tuning out my attorney, and waiting to be summoned into the courtroom where I would face a judge. I had pleaded guilty to first degree assault, a plea bargain, but my fate hung in the rafters, for I still could be sentenced to 3 to 7 years in the state prison. Some bargain!

Still, I remained calm for some reason, breathing in and out slowly.

"Nam...Myaho...Renge...Kyo," I chanted to myself with my eyes closed.

All of a sudden, I heard the sound of footsteps coming towards my attorney and I, as we waited outside the assigned courtroom where my case would be heard. I looked up to see the jailer coming.

He stopped in front of us and said, "It's time for your case."

My attorney stood up first. There were no words or eye contact exchanged between us, I just stood up and followed him into him courtroom.

The doors were opened for us by the jailer that had summoned us. My attorney held the door for me as I followed in behind him. There was a second set of doors that lead into the courtroom. This was it. There was no turning back now, no running away.

As I entered, I caught a glimpse of the Puchaz family. They had come for me. I was so very blessed with their loyalty to me through thick or thin.

Then, I noticed my brother and his wife, my cousin ,the eating disorder specialist and the counselor I had been speaking with, Eileen. They were all there, sitting and waiting for the hearing to begin.

Nowhere to be seen were the rest of my family, the people that I would do anything for: an aunt, two uncles and other cousins. If they were in my shoes, I would give them my support and love. But people can't give what they don't have.

The last two people my eyes came upon were my two daughters. My heart sank to the floor, how agonizing for them to be witness to all of this. What had I dragged them into? I had discussed with them beforehand that they did not have to come. I had apologized many times for any heartache that I had caused them before this day.

"You didn't hurt us, Mom. You hurt yourself. We are here for you. There is only one way to go, and that is up," my daughters had said to me.

I remember my eyes welling up with tears, I even laughed, as the tears rolled down my cheeks. I knew at that very moment, no matter what happened, everything was going to be all right. With the acceptance and pure love of my children, I could deal with anything!

I *had* to be strong. I could not unravel, as I followed my attorney into the court room to where we would be seated, to the right of the judge. We sat down and waited for the judge to enter. He would be announced first, of course.

You needed the patience of a saint in this tedious process, the justice system. What? Wait for this, wait for that. Enough to drive anyone insane, well, even more insane! I had already been deemed insane.

Finally, the judge was announced, and he entered.

"All rise. The honorable judge Bourque," the court security guard called out loudly.

Everyone in the courtroom rose up before this man, this judge, dressed in a long black robe. He then sat down at his enormous desk, his judgment desk. Once he was seated, we were allowed to sit. Oh, the rituals of the civilized man. And so began the hearing.

The featured guest speaker was the eating disorder specialist. It was tormenting to listen to her talk about my DISORDER. The disorder that was only the symptom of my life experiences, the traumas I had gone through.

Others spoke. I don't recall the order or the exact content of their comments. However, I do recall two people who spoke.

One was an officer from the Goffstown Police Dept., some youngster, who spoke on behalf of the law, the community. That I could have, key statement, COULD HAVE injured many people in the duplex where I resided with the predator. The place where I aimed a 38 special purchased at a gun shop in Hooksett, NH, at the violator, the predator. Five shots to be accurate, with one bullet left for me.

Not one of the bullets was a direct hit. One ricocheted, and slightly injured one of his legs.

My God, as I write the torrid details of that day, that event, I cannot believe it. For it truly seems like fiction, not fact!

The next individual to speak was the predator. He was going to speak on my, my behalf? How sweet of him. He spoke of how I was a good person. That even though I aimed a gun and shot at him, he had no hard feelings. I was very sick. The divorce, the family abandonment and the bulimia had consumed me. That he had gone out and bought a book on the illness, and was HELPING me! He did everything he could to mask his true nature.

He had helped all right, helped himself to my body, and my mind. I never gave him permission to rape me or torture me physically, or emotionally. He never heard the NO that I had screamed at the top of my lungs.

So, there it was, all my dirty laundry hanging out on the line for the world to see, to hear, in front of family, friends and the media. Yes, the media did show up!

I blocked out all the things that everyone had said in the courtroom, especially the predator's statements. All the talking became a very dull, mumbled, incomprehensible dialogue that my ears could not hear. I was in survival mode for myself.

The prosecutor, Jason Lord, spoke also. My recollection of his statement has since escaped me.

"Nam…Myaho…Renge…Kyho," I chanted to myself, over and over and over again.

I believe we had a recess at this point. We all headed outside the courtroom. The expressions of family and friends were that of shock and disbelief. I had limited eye contact, so as not to disturb my protective shield.

I headed into the ladies' room where I was met by my girlfriend Judy and her daughters, Karen and Leslie, all friends of mine. Only one of my cousins had shown up, and my most precious gifts, my two daughters.

When my cousin caught sight of me she began to sob uncontrollably.

"What the hell," I said to myself. She had never shown such emotion for me. I began to comfort her anyway.

Who was on trial here?

I couldn't help but wonder though, were these tears of sadness or tears of joy? I believe the later. Joy, that I would be punished so she would look better than me. Her story is another book. A terrible thing to say, but if they were tears of sadness, tears shed out of truly caring, I would have heard from her since then. It's been eight years, not one phone call, not one card or letter, nothing!

The truth does set you free! I was merely entertainment for the day. She put on quite a show herself.

IT WAS TIME to return to the courtroom. We all filed back in, family, friends, counselors, a prosecutor, a lawyer, and a plea bargainer. No partridge in a pear tree. All present and accounted for.

It was my turn to speak to the judge, once he asked me to make my statement. So, I chanted the sacred words to myself before I stood up.

"Nam...Myaho...Renge...Kyho."

There was certainly some divine intervention going on. For the calm that washed over me on that day was unbelievable. I was fearless, in fact. There was a connection to something far greater than anything I had ever felt on this earth, and for the first time in my life I surrendered to the pure love of my creator. I forgave my trespasses and all those who had trespassed against me. Oprah Winfrey once said, "Forgiveness is giving up the hope that the past could have been different."

Then, the judge called upon me to speak.

You could have heard a pin drop. I felt all the eyes in the courtroom staring at me, trying to penetrate through the great love shield I had surrounded myself with. All their fears were unsuccessful in melting down that shield.

I pushed back the chair that I was sitting on, and stood slowly. I took in three deep breathes, letting each one exit slowly. Those yoga classes had surely paid off. No medication necessary here!

One more time in the courtroom, I chanted to myself in the loudest voice inside my head, "Nam...Myako...Renge...Kyho."

I cleared my throat, and began.

"Your honor I appreciate this time to speak to you today. I wanted to let you know how very, very, sorry I am for what I have done. I also wanted to tell the predator that I am sorry.

"Now that I am well, I still can't believe that I did such a horrible thing. I wasn't myself."

I spoke as calmly as I could. All the words were from my truth, so I had no problem.

I continued.

"There were many mental pressures that I was unable to control. I was wrong to let fear, guilt and shame control me.

"While at Valley St. Jail, I had a lot of time to think. Sometimes, we were locked up for 22 hrs, in a 7 x 13 cell. I decided I needed to GET IT.

"Since I was released in August 2001, on my own, I have arranged for counseling, and done counseling, and worked.

"For the first time in my life, I am in the driver's seat. I am in control," I stated ever so calmly, ever so smoothly.

I continued, "My daughters and I are closer than ever. The divorce had caused us to become distant. This is my greatest gift! I have no expectations from anyone but myself. I want to extend my thanks to the prosecutor, and the head of the probation department for their time with my case, and for seeking out the truth."

That was all there was to say, and I sat back down in my chair.

THE COURT ROOM was hauntingly quiet now, as everyone waited for the verdict. My verdict!

My recollection of the exact words of the judge has become a bit clouded. However, this is what I do recall. I was waiting in the chair that I had been sitting in through the whole courtroom scene.

Once again, I began to chant the words loudly inside my head like the beating of a drum, "Nam…Myako…Renge…Kyho," over and over. Within a few minutes we were asked to stand.

We, meaning my attorney and I, to the right facing the judge, and on the left side, facing the judge, was the prosecutor.

I was holding back a deluge of emotions, trying to maintain my composure, no matter what the judge would sentence me to. I could not become unglued in any way, especially in the presence of my daughters.

Then, the judge's words passed through his lips as I listened intently to his judgment of me, and my behavior.

The judge said a lot of things. As I stated before, I don't recall most of what he said. All except the following.

"You will serve three and a half years." Everything else was just noise to me, with no disrespect to the judge.

"Oh my God," was my immediate reaction. "NO, NO, NO!" My mind racing, screaming inside me, trying very hard to understand what I had heard. My body felt like it had been slammed by a bulldozer as I leaned on my attorney for support. I felt as though I was going to fall to the floor.

My attorney held my left arm tightly by the elbow and supported my frail body so I wouldn't fall over.

"Listen," he commanded, in a soft tone into my left ear. It was inaudible to anyone else in the courtroom but me, but he had grabbed my attention, and I listened.

As an extraordinary miracle would have it, it turned out that the three and a half years was in regards to probation. PROBATION!

Yes, I was sentenced to three and a half years on probation. Not three and a half years at the women's state prison, in Goffstown, NH.

I had never once since all the craziness had started in June of 2001, entertained the idea of being in prison. For, I had already served my time while living in the clutches of the predator, and in the homes I had lived in as a child.

Quiet sighs of jubilation escaped into the room.

"Oh my God, oh my god and Thank you, thank you,' were the words swirling around inside my head, too. We were all overcome with pure joy and disbelief as well.

MY ATTORNEY QUICKLY escorted me into a room off the courtroom. He felt that if would be better if everyone cleared out before I headed out, especially the predator!

In a lecturing fashion, he educated me on the conditions of my probation, about the seriousness of probation, and the need for strict adherence to every single order.

Leslie, my friend, was summoned into the room a short while later. I would be calling her home my home, until I could afford a place of my own. She, too, was told of the rules and regulations, and of her role in this process, and reminded of my bulimia illness. All of this was for a journey to a better place, yet I felt naked and exposed.

"This too shall pass," I repeated to myself over and over again inside my beautiful mind. Everything was going to be all right, everything!

Enough time had passed for most of the people to file out of the courtroom. The media from the channel nine news station were still lingering around, waiting for a statement from me. I believe I was asked something to the effect of, "Was justice served today?"

"Yes," I answered, "YES."

In the lobby, on the first floor, my friends Karen, Leslie ,Judy, and her family, my two daughters, and my brother and his wife were waiting.

I gave each one of them a hug and expressed my gratitude for being there for me.

"Let's go celebrate at Puritan Back Room," I said, "the meal is on me!"

I lead the way out.

I was so overcome with joy, that as I got outside onto the sidewalk, I knelt down and kissed the ground. My daughter came rushing over to my side. She thought that I had tripped and fallen.

"Are you all right, Mom?" She asked.

"Yes," I said. "I just had to kiss the ground. All this is finally over."

Everyone laughed.

"Come on," I said. "Let's go celebrate!"

Then we headed for the restaurant in Manchester. I drove myself there in my white Chevy S-10 pick-up truck.

I had no job; I had been let go from my place of employment, a dry-cleaning business in Hooksett. I had about two hundred dollars in the bank, a place to live, a pick-up truck, the love of my two daughters and close friends, and enough love and hope in my heart to help me carry on. And with my invisible ruby red slippers, I did.

ONCE WE WERE all seated at the Puritan restaurant, and everyone had ordered their beverage of choice, I said in an overly joyous tone, "I would like to make a toast. To justice, and the love and support of you all, thank you!"

My eyes became moistened with tears as I raised my glass high. All present did the same, and then we brought our glasses to our lips, and we drank. Triumph over tragedy, for this mountain anyway. Not knowing at that time that there would still be more to come. But, at least the Everest Mt. of my life had been conquered!

"Home is where the heart is," they say. I still wasn't quite yet there. For there was more learning to do. It seems so easy to say that there is "No place like home," like Dorothy had said. I didn't know HOME totally yet for my soul.

The Puritan celebration lasted for a couple of hours. That frozen, foggy feeling was still lingering. Thank God too, for ever since I left the courtroom, I wanted to purge up all the pent-up emotions, mostly the deep down joy. I felt that the display of true joy, however, would not be a very good idea, it might seem like I got away with something. So, it remained tucked away until I could freely let it out. In the cab of my truck, alone, would be perfect.

Tight embraces were given to all those who had accompanied me to the restaurant.

My truck was waiting for me in the parking lot. I unlocked the door, entered, and closed the door behind me. I rolled down the window on the driver's side and just sat there for what seemed like forever. It was very hot, but it felt so good. I was living now, not just existing!

I felt safe here inside the cab, and if this cab could talk, oh, the stories it could tell! All true of course, life in all its full living color. The seat supported my frail body like a pair of comforting arms of an old friend. Then all of a sudden, as if given permission, the floodgates opened wide, and I allowed myself to feel all of the emotions that I had been holding back. Just because you are brave doesn't mean that you don't cry.

I felt all the essence of pure joy, and all the agony of the sorrow. I put my arms on the steering wheel and folded them at the elbows, then rested my head inside the rectangular opening. I sobbed uncontrollably for a long while.

I never let myself become the victim, for a brief moment maybe, way back in the summer of June, 2001. However, I would never allow myself to let the acid victim mentality consume me totally! I always had my pride. No one can ever take that away from you. You need to rise to the occasion no matter how battered, bruised, or broken you are, and I did!

"Stronger and still standing," as I had heard quoted from the movie *Antoine Fisher.*

AND ON ONE particular day a silent moon had rumbled the truth into the heart of one in charge. And in the name of the love of Kathleen Rioux, a sentencing had been set forth.

It wasn't the golden harvest moon, or the brilliant blue moon, or even the banana shaped quarter moon. Oh no, it was the beautiful, mighty Thunder Moon.

And the Thunder Moon waxed and waxed and waxed!

PART TWO:

BROKEN SMILE

Broken Smile

A smile is so
so much more
than teeth,
crooked or cracked,
discolored or white
or missing.
A smile is,
so much more
than lips,
full or thin,
pink or red.
A smile is a force,
an energy,
a joy,
and even though
it may be broken,
it shows the world
a love of just being

THIRTY

In the last scene of the movie, *The Wizard of Oz*, the balloon that was to carry Dorothy and the Wizard back to Kansas accidentally comes loose. As Dorothy steps out of the basket to retrieve Toto, off drifts the balloon, and Dorothy is left behind in the city of Oz to carry on. A frantic Dorothy, the scarecrow, the tin man and the lion suddenly notice a beautiful pink bubble floating towards then. Behold, it's Glinda, the good witch of the north!

When Dorothy asks Glinda for help, Glinda tells her that she's always had the power to go back to Kansas. Then she asks Dorothy what she has learned.

Dorothy responds that, if she's ever going to look for her heart's desire again, she won't look any further than her own backyard! Because if it isn't there, she never really lost it to begin with.

Glinda: That's all it is. Now, those magic slippers will take you home in two seconds. Are you ready? Close your eyes, and tap your heels together three times and think to yourself, there is no place like home, there is no place like home. THERE IS NO PLACE LIKE HOME!

WEEKS PRIOR TO the court date, I had asked my childhood friend since the third grade, Leslie, if I could move into her home providing the verdict was probation. She agreed without hesitation, other than to ask her husband.

I was truly astounded by her kindness and generosity! I wish I would have gone to her initially when I was engulfed in all the madness. Oh no, it was all for a reason, a good reason for sure. For the place I am at now, yes, I would do it all again.

Anyway, I regained my composure as I drove back to my brother's home. I went there to collect the belongings I had left there. Some clothes, books, the cot that I had slept on for almost a year, and some other odds and ends.

Thanks goodness for my pick-up truck! I would be able to pack everything up into one load. I couldn't get out of there quickly enough. The torment of my living situation at the time had finally come to an end.

I experienced what I did. However, I do not hold any grudges, really. For we need to, "Forgive us our trespasses, as we forgive those who trespass against us," and I did.

It was another opportunity to grow, I guess, to pay attention and look at myself. So I would never, ever, be back to this place again. For I had thrown away my peace and my serenity, and I was going to get it back! I could never love anyone at my expense again!

As I drove into the driveway, I noticed that both vehicles were parked inside the two stall garage. I took a deep breath as I opened the door of my pick-up truck, got out and closed the door. I headed up into the house through the garage door entrance. One last time to deal with their ways, their discontent, I thought.

The house was hauntingly quiet as I entered. Maybe everyone was outside in the backyard, I secretly hoped.

I was greeted with a "Hi," from my sister-in law, as I passed through the kitchen, and headed upstairs toward the room to my bedroom. When I reached the second floor, I turned to the left and entered my room. I packed up all my belongings. Definitely five trips to my pick-up truck I accessed, as I looked around the room.

I lifted two of the boxes, took a right, and headed toward the stairway. The hallway also had the opening to my brother Jim and his wife's master bedroom, which was to my left, as I approached the top of the stairs.

The door to their bedroom was open, and as I passed by, I could see my brother sitting up on his bed. His back was resting on the head board, his legs stretched out in front of him.

He was just sitting there. The expression on his face was not one of joy or happiness. It was a look of shock, and almost disappointment. It was only a surface wound. Fortunately for me, I looked away quickly before his fear arrow pierced my heart. A technique I learned from years of experience of living with troubled people. They try to make you feel lower than them so that they can feel higher, better. But, when you live in fear that is what you attract.

Disappointed that I wasn't going to prison, perhaps. Maybe that he didn't have control of me or the situation. He wouldn't be able to visit me at his convenience, like the relationship we had shared with our mother when she was institutionalized. Once again, we do the best we can with what we know.

They didn't know it, but if the verdict would have been incarceration, my whole family would have found themselves unable to visit me. I would have forbidden it. But they might not have wanted to come anyway.

I know now how juvenile that reaction was. However, it was some sort of self-preservation thing for sure, purely ego, but oh so freeing. They had turned their backs on me. At that time, they were as toxic as the predator.

This is all history of course, the sting of their abandonment gone. Once again, people cannot give what they do not have. I understand it now, I do.

So, in no time, the truck was loaded up and I was headed to my next temporary home, in Manchester, NH.

It truly doesn't matter how well you know someone, once you live with them all their idiosyncrasies come spilling out onto the floor, like M&M candies, when you open the bag the wrong way. I include myself in this spillage.

It's as if the glue we use to hold ourselves together in the way we want the world to see us as melts away, and leaves us standing naked and exposed in our kitchens. Only to prepare dinner for the ones who really know you and love you anyway, well hopefully.

WITHIN A FEW weeks I had settled in, and quickly learned the dynamics of the Peterson household. I learned how each family member interacted with one another, and how I needed to fit into their daily life.

I tried to make myself as scarce as possible, wanting to be transparent at times. You can't take anything personally; you go with the flow. After all, you are the new kid on the block. This is not just about your behavior at the playground. It's about the day to day living that requires inner strength.

My bedroom was the computer room, and would remain available for any family member whenever they needed to use the computer. I had to accommodate the flow of traffic into the room whenever someone wanted access. I learned to become extremely flexible.

I reminded myself to be grateful every single day. It kept me centered, sane.

ON NOVEMBER 13, 2002 my father died. His death was really a relief for me, sorry to say. But every visit to the nursing home, the VA in Manchester, NH, left me beaten down. I couldn't see a once vibrant father, totally immobilized and bed ridden. Dependent on others to feed him, dress him and yes, to change him because he couldn't use the bathroom.

It was ironic that a man like my father, who was an alcoholic, raging at times, had survived binges, detoxification, hit and runs and now, couldn't rise above this mere stroke. I angrily waited for him to suddenly rise up from his bed, and be healed. Like all the other times that it seemed like he had risen from near death situations.

Not this time though, not this time.

I cried bitterly for him, once I hung up the phone that night. I cried for him, not for me. I cried for the life he didn't live.

"I love you, Dad. I wish you peace," I whispered to myself.

We planned a mass at Our Lady of Perpetual Help church, on the east side of Manchester a few days later. It was the same church where our mother's funeral had been held.

I wanted to speak on his behalf. To say something that he would be remembered by, something that testified that his existence was important, that some part of him, just him, was left behind.

So in the confines of my bedroom/computer room, in the home of the Peterson family, I racked my brain to come up with a fitting eulogy for my dad.

I thought about a lot of things. Some good, mostly not so, but then all of a sudden, it came to me as clear as a cloudless sky in autumn. Something I remembered he really did live by. A saying he had once asked me to write down for him, in calligraphy, on an unlined piece of white paper. And then to frame it, so that he could hang it up in the kitchen on Frontage Road.

I was so touched at the time, as I remember back how I felt when asked. Apparently, he did admire my artistic abilities.

I am not sure if this saying was an original one, thought up by my father. There were glimmers of insightfulness. However, I do believe that he probably read it somewhere, and was moved enough to feel it was frame worthy, for it truly did sum up how he lived his life, like it or not.

It went like this: *Happiness is being what you want to be, not what someone else wants.* And with those very words, I ended his eulogy. I returned to the pew and sat down by my daughters and my brother Jim, as the song we chose played in the background. "In the Arms of the Angels," by Sarah McLachlan, and that is where, I believe, he is right now.

I vividly recall, while driving to the cemetery, feeling so beaten down by life, and living. I thought of the seemingly endless parade of pain in childhood, about my choices to marry, divorce and then to unconsciously choose a heinous predator to involve myself with, only to leave with a felony charge, and now, the death of my father.

I thought I had followed all the rules growing up, always trying to do good, better, loving everyone without any conditions. Yes, continually loving at my expense. What did I expect?

Suddenly, the burden of everything felt like a 100 lb weight on my chest, I could barely breathe.

I was suffocating, the WHY ME question almost shooting out of my mouth like a flame.

It was at that very moment that the WHY turned into "God, are you there? Please show me a sign, something, to let me know that everything is going to be all right." It was an urgent, desperate, inner voice.

With my face turned toward the window, looking out at the scenery, then up into the cloudy gray sky, tears slowly rolled down my cheeks. No one to witness the agony of my hopelessness, thank goodness. I wouldn't want to appear weak.

As I continued my gaze upward, all of a sudden, the clouds parted, and there it was, the sign, this small patch of brilliant bright blue sky! I smiled on the inside and the outside as well. I sniffled, and quickly brushed the wet from my cheeks.

My faith was restored. I believed everything was going to be all right! We just need reminders every now and then. And we do get them, if we ask.

MY FATHERS PASSING left my brother and I with some funds. We were granted a small portion of the estate, a gift, if you will.

I had relocated to 3 Oakwood Lane in November of 2002. It was the home of a college friend, Barbara Herman. I was able to have my own room there. Barbara had a condo, and lived alone.

Leslie and her family were gracious, but this new arrangement would allow Leslie and her family to resume their lifestyle, and I would have more space.

I was very grateful for my friends welcoming into their homes, but I yearned for my own space and place. My own home! Fortunately, by December of 2002 I was granted a sum of money which enabled me to seek shelter elsewhere.

Next stop in my nomadic journey was Sagamore Street in Manchester. It was a one bedroom apartment on the third floor. It was small, but it was my place, my space to do whatever I wanted to do. Sing in, dance in, clean in, and to entertain in. And to walk around however I dam well pleased in, and prepare the meals I wanted, and cleaning up afterward was simply optional!

So, with the first month's rent and a security deposit, I signed a lease. I'll have to say, I was feeling on top of the world. I was making my way towards regaining my independence, getting my life back! It was a zig zag sort of route, but a route nonetheless.

Once the rental agent had gone, I held out my left hand, the hand with the keys to my new pad, my home, in it. I slowly unfolded my fingers and there they were. Two very tarnished gold keys, one key for the front entrance and the other for my apartment, and they were real. This was not a dream!

I sat down on the hardwood floor of my tiny unfurnished living room/dining area. I pulled my knees into my chest, rested my head on my knees, and wept. Happy tears, and grateful sobs.

And I moved forward with a broken smile, and invisible ruby red slippers on

TWENTY-FOUR

I WAS MOVED into the apartment within a few weeks. I didn't have all my belongings back yet. Mr. predator had decided to put the things I had left behind into storage for me. Without anyone's permission of course. He was looking to collect about $3000.00 to have my things returned, my attorney Mr. Swope had informed me.

I mean, come on. Pay someone for what he did to me, for breaking the law! Or better yet, really fucking you over, I don't think so! So, I let Mr. Swope know that the predator could keep my things, and to stick them, well, you know where.

I dealt with *that* blow from the predator by telling myself, "What if you had been in a fire, and you had lost everything?" So, with that in mind, I let go of those thoughts, the sentimental ones, about belongings, pictures and clothes. It was just stuff! I still had myself. I was stronger and still standing!

So I settled in joyfully into my new third floor dwelling. I was working at Euro Dry Cleaners, in Bedford, NH at the time, working as much as I could, often six days a week. Really, anything to keep my home, my studio apartment, at $675.00 per month, heat included.

My rate of pay was $8.00 per hour. However, if I worked on Saturdays, I could make time and a half, which was $12.00 per hour. WOW, poverty level or what?

Did you know that if you make under $18.00 per hour, you are living at the poverty level? Imagine all the people working for that amount and trying to make it. It's simply mindboggling!

Anyway, up until now I had never lived alone. I had lots of healthy distractions, my running, hiking, biking (not on a motorcycle) and my art interests. I even volunteered at the Palace Theatre as an usher for evening shows.

You don't realize how deeply things can stay with you, though. How the horrific events of the past are not always far enough behind, and in the darkness, those terrifying memories creep up and crawl into bed with you. The passing of time is the healer. The memories never leave you totally, but their impact on you lessens.

The trigger can be a movie. For example, I innocently thought that I could watch a movie like *Sleeping with the Enemy*, and not be hurled back to it all! Like it's happening all over again in full living color, the verbal abuse, emotional abuse and rape.

When you live alone there is simply nothing to distract you sometimes in the middle of the night, as you lay in your bed, in your apartment. Your mind regurgitating the poison that you were force-fed in the past, leaving your in full fetal position on the floor, crying and screaming, as you try to comfort yourself.

You don't call anyone because you should be able to deal with all this. Shame and guilt stand over you like a disappointed adult, so you don't call. You were never consoled growing up anyway.

"It's all right. It's all right. It was just a nightmare. It's over. He's not here." You rocked yourself back and forth, back and forth, in the arms of an angel that you believed had adopted you.

It was years before I could watch that movie.

The sight of the predator's truck and license plate was another great obstacle that eventually I had to overcome, too. It had the same, down on the floor, fetal position, effect on me. I was very gentle with myself, it was okay, I felt what I felt. Time does heal everything as long as you let it, I believe, and you live in the moment.

At the time I was also involved with Gary Tardie. I had met him while under the roof of my brother Jim and his wife Pam. Needless to say, he was a godsend of sorts. Well, for providing me with the key to his place to go to whenever I needed a haven from my hell.

"Reasons, seasons, lifetimes," a close friend of mine, Mike, always says.

The hiccup part of the relationship was that he was using me because he had lost his license from a DWI. His son had been in the car when he was arrested, therefore making it a felony. Imagine that, just two felons, hanging out together, one using the other. Now isn't that a Hallmark card moment?

I had my own place, but at times it did not provide me with comfort as I had wished it would. All the reality came crashing down at times, and with nobody around as a buffer, I had to face the reality of my own company.

I was still on probation, too. You never knew when they would spring an unannounced visit on you, just to check on you. To see how you were doing.

Yah, right!

The visit was with the clear intention of bringing you down, of finding something to incarcerate you for. My probation officer, along with some other sidekick probation officer, a young future thug officer, could come at any time.

Once, they arrived at about 10pm. I was in bed, dressed in nothing more than my underwear.

I woke from a deep sleep to the sound of the door buzzer, it buzzed, didn't ring. It was located on the first floor. My apartment was on the third floor. I jumped out of bed half asleep, scared to death with no idea of who might be calling at this hour. Remember, third floor, you can look out your window, but you can't see who it is!

I grabbed my long sleeve shirt and sweatpants that were on the end of the bed, and threw them on. Then I slipped on my clogs, opened the door, and headed to the first floor to see who was there.

The hallway wasn't well lit, so I hung onto the banister for support and descended cautiously, as I was becoming more awake with each step down. No, this was not a dream. I could still hear the sound of the buzzer coming from my apartment, the noise growing fainter as I reached the second floor landing, then the first floor.

The heavy wooden ornate door had a thick glass window in the center, so you could see who had come a calling at this ungodly hour. I saw them before they saw me, and once I recognized my probation officer's face, I was both relieved and extremely annoyed at the same time. The relieved part opened the door and graciously offered them to come in, like I had any other option.

It was at times like this that I reminded myself to get it and to stay clear of the system. They come into your home, full of intimidation, and try to scare the shit out of you.

It seemed to me that their intent was to make you fail, not succeed at this game, their game actually. Each PO playing by his or her own set of rules. You just went along with whatever it was that they said. They needed to believe that they were in control.

So, in they stormed. Like I was doing something I shouldn't. There was my probation officer checking my cabinets in the pantry, looking in the refrigerator, while her accomplice went from room to room turning on light switches, trying to find something, anything to bring me into jail. Not tonight people, not tonight!

My probation officer's demeanor was so condescending. It was probably a learned response from years of being a PO, like a protective shield. She treated me like I was below her, and would never be equal. Her body language and the way she spoke to me reeked with disrespect. It's no wonder some criminals ever rose above their labels, they were led to believe, by the treatment they received, that's all they were.

Somewhere, I believe, my probation officer had been hurt, traumatized even, and she was using her position to make others hurt too.

Even with all the obstacles, the third floor, the working six days a week and the unexpected visits, this was still my home, MY HOME, and I wouldn't change it for anything!

IN MAY OF 2003 I walked into work the Monday after Mother's Day and my wonderful owner of Euro Cleaners in Bedford, NH had the assistant manager, Carol, let me go. You know, FIRE me! He didn't even have the balls to tell me himself. He figured I would just slink away and go home to my north end residence. Well, I didn't! I waited in my white pick-up truck for him to show up.

I was fired at 8:00am and waited until 9:00am, that's when he usually strolled in, to have a face to face with him.

The look on his face was priceless as he pulled into the parking lot in front of the shop and noticed me in my truck. He didn't get out. He just kept looking out, with a glimmer of fear in his eyes. Probably it was the idea that he was going to be confronted by a felon. Well, a retired felon.

Finally, I opened my door and headed toward his red car. I think he thought I was going to go postal again, as I could see him scanning me from head to toe, likely to see if I was concealing a weapon.

Once I reached the driver's side of the car, where he was still sitting, he turned his head forward; he couldn't even look me in the eyes. The driver's side window was opened just a crack, the smoke from his cigarette slowly drifting out and upward.

"I am very disappointed in you," I said. "You didn't even have the decency to face me yourself! I waited here to talk to you. To tell you that I did my very best for you, and that I believe you will give me a good reference, RIGHT?"

The words just flowed out of my mouth ever so smoothly, so calmly. I didn't even raise my voice. I just spoke in monotone, with no sign of any emotion. When you speak the truth, you are set free. Free from ego!

He was dumbfounded. I think he had anticipated a hysterical confrontation, hence, the cracked window. He continued to look forward. I got the impression that he was feeling very uncomfortable, busted, shall we say. Then he said, "Right." Then he rolled up the window. It was the end of the conversation.

It didn't change the fact that I was unemployed, but I said what needed to be said, because if we don't stand up for ourselves, with respect and dignity, no one else will.

I had gone through all the money from the bonds we had received from my father's estate, the gift we had received in late November, early December. The money and my paychecks were used to live on. I mean, just the necessities, my apartment, electricity, basic cable (only $12.00 a month back then) and food. No plastic surgeries, no expensive jewels or lavish trips to the islands.

ೋ

UNFORTUNATELY, IN JULY of 2003 I had to surrender once again to the situation. I could not afford to live there any longer, and through the kindness and generosity of Sr. Marguerite Gravel, a sister of the Holy Cross, it was arranged for me to live in, well, in a convent.

More to learn, I guess.

This move was a very, very difficult one. I felt as though I had gone backwards. I'd had my own place, and now circumstances beyond my control had brought me here. Here, sitting among all these boxes I had packed, on the floor, my legs stretched before me, leaning on the east wall that faced the kitchen. Asking God to grant me serenity, and for me to accept this.

I prepared for bed with my usual routine, abdominal exercises, stretches, face cleaning with Mary Kay and brushing my teeth. I turned on my CD player, and placed my Enya CD into the slot, and I was slowly lulled to sleep. Breathing in and out, in and out, lying on the twin sized mattress and drifting far away from all of this in my dreams.

I did not know what would lie ahead, but sometimes I think that can be a good thing. I did not want to waste any energy on resisting what life had given me, for I could always choose how to deal with life.

So with the road ahead, I laughed at myself, and I went to live on Wedgewood Lane, in Manchester, NH, still Kathleen. A runner, a hiker, a mother, a sister, an aunt, a friend, a single writer on probation, with a sense of humor intact and my invisible ruby red slippers.

TWENTY-FIVE

WHEN I WAS a sophomore at Memorial High School in Manchester, NH, I used to go on retreats. I was seriously considering becoming a cloistered nun.

The Precious Blood Monastery, on Bridge Street, in Manchester, was the place to go if you were contemplating such a calling. Retreats were a way of familiarizing yourself with the daily life of this particular type of religious order.

It was so peaceful there, with your day consisting of an early morning mass, prayer sessions throughout the day, and your regular mealtimes. Oh yes, you would also meet with the Mistress of Novices and have a serious chat as to why you wanted to enter this life of silence, prayer and complete seclusion from the world.

I'll have to say that is was very appealing to one who lived in utter dysfunction. I mean with alcoholics, violence, neglect, and physical and mental abuse. Going here to this place, this wonderful, orderly, peaceful haven, well, it seemed like heaven on earth to me. An escape, and a wonderful one at that!

I never did enter. The Mistress of Novices gently told me that this was not the place for me. That I loved it here because it offered me some solace from my home life, and that in our conversations it seemed to her that I was an adventurous, social type, deep down. Entering here would like running away from life.

The Mistress of Novices was so right!

Apparently, my soul wanted me to experience that setting again, to validate my choice, from many years ago, not to become any type of nun. So, in July of 2003 I shared a house with two sisters of the Holy Cross, Sister Vivian and Sister Florence.

About a month prior, proper introductions had been made at the home, courtesy of Sister Margarite.

To refresh your memory, Sister Margarite was the nun who I had befriended at the Valley St. Jail while I was incarcerated for 55 days. I really do not think I could have survived that particular ordeal without her guidance and support.

Before moving in I had to be approved by the two elder sisters. After all, I would be their housemates, and they needed to feel totally comfortable with me, considering my felony and all. Honestly, I didn't blame them one little bit!

I did pass the test, but there was a list of stipulations, rules if you will. Meant to protect them and give them the upper hand it this situation. And for any reason if it was not working out for them, they could terminate the living arrangements at any time.

So, under my homeless circumstances, I had to once again perform the "Good Little Girl" routine. Not as to say that I wasn't capable of being respectful, sensitive or flexible, because I was. I wouldn't have made it this far, believe me. However, when you are desperate, you can lower yourself, bring acceptance, just to have a roof over your head.

It was early on that I learned the rules. Their rules, and there was no compromising at the convent whatsoever! Certain times to cook, clean, do your laundry, shower.

I finally came to the realization that they were trying to regain their power, their control, through trying to control others. They had followed all the rules for a very long time, so it was my turn, in their eyes. I did not condone their behavior, well it was primarily Sister Vivian who was on a major power trip, but I did understand it.

The irony was that the very place I thought I would find the most solace was where I found the very least. I learned that just because they had become nuns who wore habits, and had taken vows of poverty, chastity and obedience, that they were still just people. People like you and me with similar hopes, dreams and fears.

Yes, Sister Vivian and Sister Florence were humans, beings with frailties. They were doing the best they could with what they knew.

Unfortunately, many humans that wear habits, or uniforms for that matter, start to believe how we treat them, like they are better than us. But of course, they are not.

IN OCTOBER OF 2003 I spotted the predator on Mammoth Rd., in Manchester. I was on my way to meet some friends at the YMCA. We were going to carpool to the Applefest Half Marathon, in Hollis, NH.

I was headed north, slowing down for the red light at the intersection of Mammoth Rd. and Lake Ave., when I noticed it, the big black vehicle he drove, parked to my left by the park there.

My freak antennas were on alert immediately. Luckily, I hadn't stopped directly alongside of his vehicle. I would remain somewhat composed until I could read the license plate. As my truck was idling, I quickly glanced at the license plate number.

I read it, it was his. It was the predators!

My PTSD began to cover me slowly like a deep freeze, the feet came first, as the chill began to work its way up to my knees. I didn't want to panic now, I was driving. So I just kept breathing in and out, in and out, deeply, flight mode trying to win over. I remained as calm as I could, determined to reach my destination, and to get as far away from the predator as possible. When I looked out my rearview mirror, I noticed something.

"Oh my god, he's following me," I cried out inside my truck.

It was so disturbing! "Why are you doing this to me? Just leave me alone!" I called out, while continuing to drive. I was shaking now, but I did not want to pull over. I wanted to make it to the YMCA.

Once I reached the corner of Bridge and Elm Streets, I got into the left lane so that I could turn. I anxiously gazed out the rearview mirror and noticed that he was in the lane that would continue straight over the bridge, and that there were cars in front of him.

Would he switch lanes when the light turned green? Who knew! I just needed to be someplace safe. I would call the police if he continued to follow me.

That red light was the longest one of my life, and after what seemed like forever, it finally turned green. I made the left-hand turn, and then continued south on Elm Street. I noticed that I was going a bit too fast for a city street, but who cared. It might be a good thing for the police to pull me over.

I put my directional on to make a right turn onto Mechanic Street, where the YMCA was located. And as I did, I checked my rearview mirror once again. To my great relief, the predator was nowhere in sight.

I was so relieved that I began to hyperventilate and to shake uncontrollably.

As I passed by the YMCA on my left, I could see my three running buddies waiting for me. I was on time, but they had arrived a little early.

I waved as I passed by them, and gave them a fake smile. I just couldn't fall apart here, now! I just couldn't.

Once my truck was safely parked in the parking garage across from the Y, I calmed myself down with my own inner voice, my own words. In chant like fashion, sitting up straight and holding onto the steering wheel with a death grip I said, "You are all right. You are all right. He can't hurt you anymore."

I repeated the words over and over again until I actually believed them. You know that moment, when you actually believe what you are telling yourself, when your heart and your mind are one.

"You are not going to stop me from doing this race! You do not have any power over me anymore." I took in a few more deep breaths, grabbed the bag of things I was bringing along to the race, locked up my truck and was off.

At the front of the YMCA there they were, the three other runners I would be driving with. I had composed myself almost completely by the time I had reached them. He had bruised my spirit, but he had not broken it! Applefest Half Marathon here I come!

The road trip and the race went pretty well. That night however, the demons came out to try to break me again. Distractions can only do so much. PTSS was on its zig zag path, not a linear one.

So, with a broken smile, and my invisible ruby red slippers on, I would move along into the next chapter of this journey.

TWENTY-SIX

THE FRESHER the wound you received stitches for, the more easily it can become injured again, open up, and begin to bleed. It takes deeper wounds even longer to heal, and the same holds true with issues of traumatic experiences.

I had made great strides overall in the trauma of the rape and drugging ordeal inflicted on me by the predator, but this situation had catapulted the fear back into my bloodstream once again.

I just couldn't keep it to myself. Was he stalking me? I had to tell someone. I mean, what if he was going to, to, to KILL me? Not telling had gotten me into this predicament, but it was also terrifying too, because it meant it had actually happened. So, in the name of the love of my life, I told the people that I went to the half marathon with.

It was extremely important that I tell what happened, quickly, quietly. Right before the start of the Applefest Half Marathon, I needed to get it off my chest, so to speak, to lighten my load before the thirteen-mile trek.

The race went well. We all finished with respectable times, and the day's race experience kept everyone in a talkative mood, which worked as a great distraction from my pre-race confrontation.

It wasn't until I was in my truck, driving back to my new home, the convent, when, from out of nowhere, the flood of fear washed over me as I drove past the spot where I had spotted the predator in his vehicle. It had really happened!

It's like that gash you get on your index finger when you were chopping up onions to go into the skillet. Just when you think it has healed, you bump it on the corner of the kitchen table, and the blood begins to spill out quickly, once again requiring a band-aid. It wasn't totally healed after all.

The sighting of his vehicle had broken open the wound of sexual assault and abuse, and fear was bleeding out everywhere. The bandages of hiking, running and trying to live my best life could not withstand the greater force of Post Traumatic Stress Syndrome, and once again the wound would require immediate attention.

I was a basket case when I reached Wedgewood Lane. I parked my pick-up truck, checking my surroundings in case the predator had followed me there. Once I knew the coast was clear, I made my way up onto the porch and entered in through the front door.

I felt weighed down by the recollection of the sighting. Like my clothes were made of cement. I walked towards the couch in the den to lighten my burden. I had to sit down quickly, or I would slam down to the floor.

Sister Vivian was sitting down in her chair in the den reading, and as her eyes caught sight of me, she lowered her book down to her lap and said, "What happened to you? Are you all right?"

Unknowingly, she had asked the wrong questions for sure.

I tried very hard to remain calm, and to tell what happened with little emotion, but the storm had been brewing inside me all day long, and I erupted like a sudden severe thunderstorm on a hot humid summer day.

I should have taken a deep cleansing breath before I started to speak, but I had to regurgitate the event from my mind, or I thought I would start to crumble again!

"I saw him. He was parked on Mammoth Road, and then he began to follow me to the YMCA." I spewed out words all over the place in a shaken, tear-ridden, tormented manner. Feeling relieved and extremely frightened at the same time.

Sister Vivian had no idea what I was talking about. For my mangled gibberish madE no sense to her I am sure, as I look back.

I was unable to calm myself, now. The current of the emotional trauma I had experienced could not be contained, and I shocked my listener, Sr. Vivian, to the core. Up until this point, I had been in control of my fears. However, this trigger unleashed all the stored-up experience.

A few weeks after the incident, Sr. Margarite had called me and arranged for me to meet with her at her residence. She wanted to talk to me. And before I even got to the meeting, I knew in my gut what was about to happen.

"Sister Vivian and Sister Florence no longer feel safe with you living in the convent, their home. They would like you to find another place to live as soon as possible."

INITIALLY, IT FELT like another punch in the stomach. I felt betrayed once again. I mean, they were nuns. Where the hell was their compassion, their understanding? Wasn't it one of the vows they took, to love and protect humanity no matter what?

I allowed myself to feel everything. I began to sob uncontrollably.

Sr. Margarite put her arms around me as we sat on her couch, in her living room, the flood of emotions spilling out all over the place. She gently passed me a box of tissues. I pulled out a couple, and wiped my eyes, then my nose. And then she cradled me in her arms for what seemed like hours.

Even in the midst of another change in my life, a small part of me felt loved, and that Sr. Margarite genuinely cared about my wellbeing. Everything would be all right.

The seduction of expectations. Nuns do this, priests are like that. Fathers, mothers, sisters and brothers will be there for you, black and white thinking. For truly, at the end of the day, people, human beings, are going to do whatever the hell they want. You just can't take it personally!

My reaction to the news had come from my expectations of nuns. At the time, I couldn't understand their viewpoint at all. My thoughts were clouded with fear. Just as their thoughts were.

Now, the only person I have expectations from is myself. Well, I still get disappointed, even aggravated, but it doesn't last long.

In the Name of Love

IN SEPTEMBER OF 2003, I was at one of my favorite spots here in the queen city, Lake Massabesic. It's a wonderful little place on the outskirts of the city, so close and yet so far away from the hive of life. It's like being up in the north country without the drive.

A sanctuary of sorts, where you can trail run, mountain bike, walk, kayak, fish and sail in warmer weather. Cross country ski, snowshoe, ice skate and ice fish when the temperature goes below 30 degrees or more; a smorgasbord, certainly, for the outdoorsy individual.

So, on one such September outing there, while I was sketching, I looked up to see a gentleman approaching me. He was dressed in biking gear, shorts, T-shirt, biking gloves and a helmet. He was pushing his mountain bike alongside as he walked toward me.

I was situated up on a grassy knoll, shaded by the huge red pines that decorate the landscape across from the sandy west shore of Lake Massabesic, sitting in a beach chair. I was dressed in shorts and a sleeveless top, sipping on bottled Dasani water.

As he came towards me I took a closer look through my sunglasses. Hmm, too dark. I slowly raised them so my vision could be clearer. "Nope," I said to myself, "Nobody I know."

When he was a few feet away he said, "Hi, what are you drawing?" Great break the ice introduction, I thought to myself.

"Hi," I said back. "Just sketching the beautiful scenery here. What a great place to be on such a lovely day!"

The conversation continued on, and I learned what his name was. Also, that he was an accounting professor at a local university. He was in the National Guard as well, and was 58 years old. Trying to win over one of the female persuasion, me, he was sharing details of himself like I had slipped him some truth serum.

All during the conversation he never took off his biking helmet. So, I couldn't really tell what he looked like, and I was wicked curious! And, I wouldn't find out until our date.

Anyway, besides the personal info, we also discussed our interests and hobbies. He seemed at that time to be intelligent, well mannered, and to have a good sense of humor. All the things that truly matter in a sustainable relationship.

We really did seem to connect. My interest in him was sparked, and before I knew it, I had agreed to meet him at the 99 restaurant across from the Mall of NH, in Manchester, for a date.

I was flattered by the attention of a male, and in my own handling of the interaction. I knew he liked me, but at that time I wasn't at the point where I asked myself the critical question, "Do I like him?"

This encounter had occurred on a Tuesday, and the date and time was set for the upcoming Thursday evening. I had plenty of time to pick out the perfect outfit! So, let the planning begin!

When I arrived back at the house, I told Sr. Vivian about my new friend and the plans we had made for our first date.

"Remember the last man you had in your life and what he did to you," she was quick to remind me. "I don't want you to go with him. You don't even know him. Anything could happen to you!" Her voice was filled with grave concern.

"He seems fine. He's a professor at a local university, he's in the National Guard and athletic too," I stated strongly, trying to defend my decision, deflecting the unsolicited advice being hurled at me.

"Well, if you insist upon this date, let me at least have a background check done on him first. I have a friend who can provide this service for me, all right?" Sr. Vivian asked persuasively. Although I felt that is was more of a command than a question.

When I looked into her eyes, I could see that her intent was indeed to protect me, so I agreed.

"Yes, go ahead. I need all the help I can get, with my track record."

Wow! The power of a nun, they reign in heaven and on earth!

So, Sr. Vivan had the background check done by the next day, amazingly! And Mr. Massabesic passed the test, and in a strange way, I was so grateful she had done that for me. The Thursday encounter was on. I would get dressed up in my favorite light gray pants and my sheer blue and red floral printed blouse, with a broken smile and ruby slippers, and go on my date.

⁂

THURSDAY EVENING FINALLY arrived. I was, I'll have to admit, excited about going on a date. It had been awhile. The background check was actually a confidence booster, to be honest!

At 5:45pm I said my good-byes to Sister Florence and Sister Vivian and headed to the 99 Restaurant to meet Mr. Massabesic. I was interested, let's face it. I mean, the possibility of a real man in my life was intriguing. Well, and the part about him being in the National Guard.

He had described his car in the last conversation we had had. It was an older car, one of those big boat types. The make and model escapes me. I, in turn, had told him what I would be driving. My white pick-up truck, of course.

At precisely 6:00pm I pulled into the parking lot. Immediately, I spotted the big car and parked up alongside it. Both vehicles were facing the same direction. I put the truck into first gear, turned off the truck, and secured the emergency brake. I then placed my keys into my purse, along with my Ralf Lauren sunglasses, looked over my left shoulder and waved hello.

As I glanced, I could hardly believe my eyes. I actually blinked a few times to make sure the setting sun wasn't distorting my sight.

There, in all his elderly looking glory was Mr. M. I mean, he looked like my, my grandfather! He was bald on the top of his very round head, and the hair that he did have, mostly on the sides, was white. He also had a strange resemblance to that jolly old elf, no disrespect intended. I like Santa.

The thought that was now swirling around in my head like a whirlpool, in a childlike taunting voice was, "Nah, Nah, you should have had him take off his bike HELMET," over and over again, louder and louder.

"You cannot judge a book by its cover," I told myself in a bold voice. Just give him a chance. So, I swallowed hard, took a deep breath, and fumbled with my keys for a moment.

I could just drive off and leave him in the dust. But instead, I thought about what I should do, opened my truck door, and stepped out.

We met each other between our two vehicles, and proceeded towards the front door of the restaurant.

He ordered wine with the meal, once we were seated. I couldn't have any wine, I was still on probation at the time. Thank goodness too, I might have done something I would have truly regretted. I was still in my, "I need a males attention mindset." And besides, I get tipsy just smelling wine!

THE DINnER WENT well. Good food and nice ambiance at the restaurant. Our conversation flowed smoothly. We laughed and seemed to connect on some levels. Our Catholic upbringings gave me a sense of security on morals and values, a false one that is.

He claimed to be active, but I had a difficult time believing that with the round little belly, that shook when he laughed like a bowl, well, you know the rest.

He took my hand as we made our way out of the restaurant. Still hoping that this might work out, I agreed to another date. He suggested we take a ride somewhere, but I said I had to get back home.

During out dinner date I had informed Mr. M. of my living situation in the convent, with the sisters. I put it more as an affordability issue, leaving out details that I decided were really none of his business at this point.

When we reached our vehicles, he gave me a hug and tried to land a kiss on my lips. However, as his face came closer to mine, I turned my head and the kiss landed instead on my left cheek. Whew!

"Good night. I had a nice time. I'll call you to see where and when you'd like to go out again," he said in an excited tone.

"Thank you. I had a nice time too. All right, call me. Goodnight," I said politely.

He got into his big old car. And I got into my truck. Off we went into the wild blue, well maybe gray, yonder.

IT WAS A WARM September evening. So, I had selected a sleeveless, cream colored, mini-striped, cotton dress for my second date with Mr.

M. I would bring along a sweater just in case the night air became chilled.

At around 5:45pm both Sr. Vivian and Sr. Florence were perched in their favorite chairs in the front parlor, curious and cautious to meet the man of the hour.

The front doorbell chimed at precisely 6:00pm. Hmm, Mr. M was a prompt pursuer. I left the kitchen, where I had been waiting his arrival, and proceeded towards the front door.

Once I reached the door, I peeked through the sheer curtain that covered the window, to the left of the door, to be sure it was Mr. M.

It was him. So, I opened the door and he entered.

"Hi Kathy," he said. As he greeted me, once again he went to plant a wet kiss on my pink little lips. He missed again, and my right cheek took the hit this time.

I lead him into the parlor to where Sr. Vivian and Sr. Florence were. They were like two mother superiors waiting to give unsolicited advice to the novice, me, Kathleen Ann Rioux!

Wait just a gosh darn minute here, nuns giving secular dating advice, I thought to myself. That's like a cat trying to teach a dog to be a cat. I don't think so! Oh, wait a minute, I do live here. Here, in a convent with nuns. Never mind. I'll just go with the flow.

When we entered the room, Mr. M walked right over to each nun, as they sat stoically in their chairs. He held out his hand, and gently shook each of their hands. He quickly began to engage in a polite conversation with them, and their acceptance of him was immediate. Once he confessed to them that he was a Catholic and attended mass every Sunday, of course.

He told them everything that they wanted to hear to capture their trust, a true politician at heart. My red flag radar had not been fully activated just yet, so I couldn't pick up what was sincerity or just plain bull shit.

After the introduction was over, we said our good-byes, and were off for another dinner date. I was still dishonoring myself. Dinner dates were my least favorite thing to do! I mean I'd rather go to church, than on a dinner date.

Desperate for a man's attention, however, I didn't use my voice. Being liked was still more important than being happy, believe it or not!

Stay tuned for the real Kathleen to come out.

Dinner was, ah, dinner. The company and the conversation wasn't as good as the first date. And at times there were long moments of uncomfortable silence. I also noticed several times that he was, shall we say, undressing me with his old blue eyes.

I just now got a cold shiver running down my spine as I recalled his sick stare.

Anyway, we finished our meals and he was still insistent that we take a stroll out at our meeting place, Lake Massabesic. So, I reluctantly got into his car, and we drove toward the lake.

At the traffic circle right before you get to the lake's main entrance however, he didn't make the right-hand turn. Instead, he veered to the left, and then took the next right onto the road that ran alongside the left side of the lake.

Why are we headed in this direction? The voice inside my head was asking, in a very concerned tone, a few notches above my normal inside voice manner.

So, I used my outside voice and questioned his choice.

"Why are were going down this way?" I stated sternly, trying to hide my anxiety.

"I'm a little tired for a walk. I thought it might be nice to just park along this road and watch the sun set over the lake."

All that I could manage to come out of my mouth was, "Oh."

He pulled his car over to the right, turned it off, and then undid his seat belt. I had been looking out my window admiring the calmness of the lake, and the reflection of the setting suns colors.

Then I undid my restraint. No sooner had my seat belt been tucked neatly back into its little holder than Mr. M. lunged toward me. I didn't even have a chance to move.

His hands forcefully grabbed my shoulders and he pulled me over to his side of the car. He then began rubbing his hands down my arms and was trying to kiss me on the lips.

"Oh my god," I said to myself, my mind screaming at the top of its lungs. "What is he going to do to me?"

With all the strength I could muster, I pushed myself away from him. I landed on the passenger's side of the car, and was prepared to jump out it necessary.

Visions of my past sexual assault had been triggered. The isolation, the feeling of being powerless and abandonment were consuming me like quicksand, and it felt like I was almost up over my neck.

"Look!" I said it so loud I startled myself, as well as the driver. "Don't touch me like that. I want to go home now! I'm not interested in you like that. Sr. Vivian and Sr. Florence will be waiting for me, it's late." I figured I'd throw in the accountability part with the sisters. Like someone knew he was with me, and that he couldn't just do whatever he wanted to me.

"I find you so attractive. It's been a long while for me since I've been with a woman." I wanted to say, no kidding, but instead I chose to keep my TOUCH ME AND I'LL KICK YOU WHERE IT HURTS face on.

"I think we would be perfect for each other. I have a lot of money, and you and your daughters could come to live in my home," he rambled on.

Oh yes, I thought to myself. You forgot to mention one thing. I'd have to sleep with you!

"Don't talk to me. Just drive me home." I said in a strong monotone voice.

"I'm so sorry. I thought you were giving me signals that you like me. That's why I thought I'd make a move," he stated, defending his disrespectful behavior.

"Just because I was nice to you does NOT mean that I want to sleep with YOU," I said back, trying to remain in control.

I could see the driveway of the nun's house, now. So grateful that I had made it home! He pulled up into the driveway and put the car into park.

"Good night," I said as I quickly opened the door and got out. In speed walk fashion I went for the front door.

I did not turn around, for fear he would get out of his vehicle and try to come after me. Passed the background check my ass! Another predator, out there on the loose, an educated predator, but a predator nonetheless!

When I opened the front door, the sisters had already gone to bed. I was so relieved, and quickly ascended the stairs to my room on the right. I opened my bedroom door, then shut it ever so carefully. I didn't want to disturb the sleeping nuns. For, I was sure they would want to question me on my date.

Once safely back inside my room, I listened to see if anyone had been roused. Not a nun was stirring, thank goodness. I sat down on the floor then and began to tremble. The tears came next, as the evenings events had triggered the horrific memories for me, memories of being drugged and raped.

I rocked back and forth, back and forth, hugging myself. "It's all right. It's all right now. You are safe. You are here, in this house."

When I was finally in a better place, a calmer place, I went over to my CD player and selected one of my CDs that I did yoga to. Probably Enya, or a similar one, I don't recall. I placed the CD into the player and found my way over to my bed. I lay down, still fully clothed, covered myself with the bedspread and began to doze off. The music embracing me like the arms of a mother, stroking my forehead gently, "Hush now," it seemed to be saying sweetly. "Good night, sweet dreams my dear."

Within a few minutes I was sound asleep, far away in a dream state of escape.

MR. M. PROVED to be unworthy of my time. Oh, he apologized several times. I even ventured out for one "Last Supper," shall we say, and I did forgive him for his overzealous behavior. He was, however, believe it or not, a saving grace for me. Because when the sisters were ready to oust me he was there to rescue me.

"Reasons, seasons, lifetimes," someone once said to me. So although we were not meant to be a couple, a season or a lifetime, my relationship with Mr. M. enabled me to have a place to live, a reason for sure.

Since he was affiliated with a local college, which I will not name, he knew of a boarding house, hard to believe they still existed, where I could live.

It was certainly an interesting experience living with two nuns, sisters, and I am so grateful that I had that opportunity. For without my great crash June 2001, I would have never known about their lives on a daily basis. I know for sure now that I would not have survived the convent. I was kind of like Maria in *The Sound of Music*, not a good fit!

So, in December of 2003, I met with Kathy, the house manager. I gave her my deposit, filled out all the appropriate forms and PRESTO, I was in. The very next day I packed up my belongings once again. My new address was Walnut Street.

I did not resist the change. I embraced it, and had an understanding that this was the way it was supposed to be.

I AM NOT a prejudice person, really. However, moving into the boarding house challenged my comfort level in dealing maturely with women of different countries and cultures.

It's not that I'm closed minded, it's just that I wasn't used to being surrounded with people who were so different than me.

The smells of their cooking took some getting used to, as it simmered on the stove in our common kitchen, and then wafted up and out into the living room. Yes, there was one medium sized kitchen for about 25 women. Amazingly no one was ever injured with any sharp objects!

By the way, the smell of fish being cooked in the morning was very unsettling and unappetizing to me as well. I guess it all comes down to what you are used to.

My room was on the second floor. It was a corner room, about seven feet by seven feet, with a small bathroom to the left, which had a shower, sink and toilet. A place I would call home until June of 2005.

The room to the right of my room was occupied by a woman from Africa and her name was Daughter. She was hard to understand at first, I mean her English needed a little polishing. As time went on though, I became accustomed to her speech, and then I was able to easily understand what she was saying.

I wasn't even sure that her name *was* Daughter, until I became better at understanding her. Of course, my first question was, "Why were you called Daughter?"

Well, evidently in that part of Africa, where Daughter came from, they are named the daughter of their father's name. For example, my father's name was Ernest, so I would have been called the daughter of Ernest. The daughter part became her name, and whatever her father's name was, was dropped. Definitely different!

Daughter was a CAN at a local nursing home, with hopes of someday becoming an RN. She was an extremely strong willed individual. Demanding, often times, and I soon learned to say "No" to her many requests. There was an air of entitlement about her, but as far as I was concerned, we were all in this together. The color of my skin, olive, did not mean that I had more. Or that I could do more for her.

When I heard her call, "Katee," I listened carefully to the way in which the tone was delivered, and in that instant, I knew whether or not to open my door to her. If I didn't open the door to my room, I learned not to feel guilty about my decision. Slowly, but surely, remembering to honor what I wanted!

CERTAINLY, THE BOARDING house was like an IHOP (The International House of People), with women from Morocco, Mexico, Pakistan and even Haiti. Yes, all of us from around the world, here together under this roof. Our commonality was to be happy, healthy, prosperous women.

It took time to adjust to my new surroundings. Feeling safe was a big one, not only about your person, but your personal belongings too.

The doors to our rooms were easy to get into. The locks not really secure, and even though I didn't have much, what I had I didn't want to share, or have shared without my permission!

Within a few weeks, however, I began to put my fears aside, and I enjoyed this dwelling. I began to get to know the other women through conversation and hanging out in the common room watching television. I could see how much we were alike. Some definitely could not be trusted, as it is in the REAL world. For the most part, I felt like I was so very fortunate to have had that opportunity. The sorority experience I had never had when I attended Notre Dame College, here in Manchester, NH.

The rent was $250.00 per month, everything included. You know, heat, hot water, laundry done on site, and cable TV. Those were the days my friend, as the song goes. For, at that time, in 2003, there was nothing like that available for women who needed safe, affordable housing. Truthfully, though, it was the affordability that kept us there!

I became friendly with Najad, who was from Morocco. Her English was as broken as Daughter's, but the more we chatted, the more I was able to understand her. She was always happy, and if she gazed into my eyes and saw sadness, she would say to me, "Katee, everything is going to be all right, I promise." And I believed her.

There was also Lucy, a fascinating white woman in her early thirties, who had acquired her pilot's license while serving in the Air Force. Oh, so incredibly cool to me. I was extremely impressed because it was always something that I wanted to do.

Lucy was probably gay. Although she never formally "Came Out," shall we say.

Once, after a visit from my probation officer, the one and only Ms. Cloutier, I had become a little unglued. The visit hadn't been a good one, with Ms. Cloutier using her power to bully me for no legitimate reason whatsoever. I mean, did I chew my gum the wrong way or something? I do recall her flare for anger towards me, but I had done nothing that violated my probation agreement. It's not like I was packing a slingshot or something! Her anger was purely used to instill fear in me, hoping that I would cave. To try to break me.!

I DID NOT!

So, Lucy just happened to walk by the slightly opened door after Ms. Cloutier had exited. I was crying, trying to comfort myself. "It will soon be over," I whispered to myself. "It will soon be over. Be strong."

I grabbed some Kleenex from the box by my nightstand. I gently wiped away the tears and blew my nose. I closed my eyes and began to chant and take deep cleansing breaths.

Lucy pushed open the door slowly. "Are you all right?" she asked.

Trying very hard to compose myself, I took in another deep breath and said, "Yes, I guess so." When I looked up, she had already edged her way into my room. She came toward me, and sat right down on my bed beside me, uninvited, and began rubbing my back.

At first, I allowed her to console me, surrendering to the touch of another human being, so desperately seeking compassion and understanding. All of a sudden, I realized her true intentions as she leaned forward to try to kiss me! I lunged out of the bed like I was being shot out of a cannon.

"I'm fine. Just fine, really, thanks," my voice slightly quivering. More trauma, just what I needed to finish off the night.

In an attempt to quickly resolve the awkward situation, I said, "I just want to be alone now."

My lunge had caused her hand to abruptly drop from my back, the distance between us now growing larger, as I was stepping backwards slowly. My stomach was in knots.

"Fine," she said, sounding more disappointed than concerned. As she headed out the door I said, "Thanks again," and then quickly closed the door and locked it.

From that day on I kept my distance from Lucy. Even though I have had tumultuous relationships with men, I had not sworn them off.

CAROL WAS ANOTHER INTRIGUING woman that lived in the house. An older woman, I had guessed her to be in her late fifties, but I found out later that she was actually in her sixties.

Carol was mysterious. She did more watching and listening than she did sharing. It seemed like Carol could ask the questions to us, however, if we asked *her* something, say just something like, "Where did you grow up?" you would find her becoming almost outraged. She would get up from her perch, the tan colored couch that faced the television, and storm off to her room.

"I'm going to bed now," she would say, her words trailing behind her as she disappeared.

UNFORTUNATELY IN THE spring of 2006 the Art Institute College bought our cozy dwelling. We were ever so coldly given a letter in March stating that we needed to out, OUT, by the end of May 2006. The college would be renovating, and for safety reasons, what a crock, we had to vacate the premises. Just like that!

No mention of where we could go, who might help us to relocate. Absolutely nothing was offered, as the cold, cruel reality knocked us on our soon to be homeless asses. The almighty dollar was at stake here. Now they could charge $600.00 per room, per month, a nice plump raise of $350.00.

Five of us, four adults and one student, had no place to go. We were in dire straits as we scrambled to find a decent place to live. It would have been helpful if we were given more of a notice. Rumor had it that they, the dean and the president of the Art Institute, were well aware of the purchase, months before we were given our two month eviction notice!

SOMEHOW, WE ALL managed to secure a safe and affordable place. I myself ended up moving in with Ms. T. Real names are not given to protect the not so innocent I don't want any sort of back lash to the truth here.

Oh, Ms. T. was simply delightful as I met her and went over the do's and don'ts of sharing her house. Feeling like she was truly opening up her living space to me. So I might finally feel like I was home.

"This is going to be just great. We are just going to get along fine. My home is your home," she said to me in the sweetest of voices. That should have been the first RED flag, the sickening sugar sweetness of her tone.

Truth is you really don't know anyone until you LIVE with them!

I was in for another surprise, a challenge, really. "Never a dull moment," as someone once said. With a broken smile and ruby slippers, I was moving onto the next chapter of this journey.

IN JUNE OF 2005 I found myself back in my old east side neighborhood. Not far from 111 Young St., where I spent from about age two and half until age eight.

At Ms. T's, my bedroom was on the second floor, to the right of the stairway. I was provided with a bed, a desk and a dresser. The room was on the northeast side of the condo, with two windows, one facing the east and the other north.

It was a ten foot by ten foot bedroom, a little more spacious that my previous room. The bed was a double bed too! Ahh! Now I could spread out and not feel so cramped. It's the little things that make a difference! You just need to be reminded.

The first few months were fine. But before I knew it, the rules began to pile up, one after the other. Things like, "Take your shoes off every time you come in, and leave them to the left of the door. Don't cook anything after 6pm. You can only watch television between the hours of 10am and 10pm. The temperature cannot be put above 58 degrees during the day," and so on, and so on.

Here we go again with that good old pins and needles feeling. The ones that were all too familiar from growing up with adults just like Ms. T. Fortunately for me, knowing that Ms. T. was this type of person helped tremendously with my survival skills.

You always have to agree with the Ms.T type people. They are always going to be right, especially when you live under their roof. You humor them often, and compliment them as often as possible.

I thank my childhood for this clear understanding of "Power and Control" type individuals. As much ammunition as you think you have, however, sometimes you do run out, and things like being tired, forgiving their childish behavior, even forgetting it, can leave you naked and vulnerable with your guard down.

Sure enough, it is times like that when, WHAM, Ms. T. would hit me with another blow. "I checked the thermostat and you turned it up to 60 degrees last night. It has to be set at 55 at night! Not 60!"

"Oh, I must not have looked carefully enough when I was setting the thermostat, so sorry."

I mean the words, the untruth, just came spilling out, sliding off my tongue into the pool of sound waves. I was behaving just like a child caught with her hand in the proverbial cookies jar.

WOW! Fifty years old and I still had to deal with adults who were bullies. You've got to do what you've got to do when you are in survival mode.

What I really wanted to do was tell Ms. T off, but I couldn't. I was living under her roof, and any and all the rules were ones I had to follow! That was, of course, unless I wanted to be camped out in the back of my Chevy.

I had to bite my tongue, nod, and agree or simply apologize. This stay better be short, I mean I'm losing bits of my tongue on a daily basis!

IN JANUARY OF 2006 I ran into an acquaintance I had met at a local running club. His name was Jason, and I had actually had a few dates with him. I just wasn't into him. You know, I did not have a spark, not even a flicker.

Anyway, we got to discussing what our current lives were like. You know, our jobs, where we were living etc. I began to tell Jason more in detail about my living situation, and what it was like to be living with Ms. T, and all her interesting DOS and DON'TS.

"That sounds really crazy! You know, my roommate moved out a couple of months ago, and I was looking for someone to share the expenses of my condo. It's a two bedroom, with two bathrooms, a washer and dryer and parking. I could charge you $50.00 less than what you are paying where you're living now."

"Seriously, I just want to be in a place where I can just relax. Be myself. I am a very flexible person, and I care about being respectful, a place where I could be happy."

"Well, why don't you come over next week to take a look at the place to make sure it's somewhere you'd like to live."

"Jason, you could be a real lifesaver! I'll call you and arrange for the day and time that would be convenient, all right?"

"Sure thing Kathy, call me."

I was so overjoyed I gave him a huge hug that nearly knocked him to the ground I almost started to cry. The thought of being rescued from this torture chamber was just the answer to my prayers.

So, a few weeks later I went to check out Jason's condo, and compared to where I was living, it was like paradise. It was a three level townhouse.

The guest bedroom , a 13ft by 13ft space, would be the place where I would rest my head at the end of the day. Sweet! It was so spacious, and Jason would be working nights, I would be working days. A schedule that would afford us with having our own personal space!

In exchange for the lower rent, however, I would prepare some meals for Jason, as well as clean the two bathrooms. It all seemed doable.

"Thank you so much," I said, showering him once again with another hug.

"Oh, you're welcome. You can move in June if you'd like. I need first month's rent, and the security deposit to seal the deal."

"Thanks again," I said as I walked down the stairs to the main entrance. Jason had remained at the top of the stairs. I opened the door, then turned around to wave good-bye, I almost wanted to blow him a kiss, and I was on my way.

I was so relieved that I shouted out in my truck, with the windows closed, "Thank God." Tears of joy rolled down my cheeks, as I felt finally free to release the emotions I was feeling. I was so hopeful that I would have peace, happiness and joy now.

In March of 2006 I moved in with Jason.

With a broken smile and invisible ruby red slippers.

TWENTY-SEVEN

I SURE KNOW how to attract the most bizarre individuals for sure. I guess, "Desperate times call for desperate measures." You'd think that by now I would be off the hook with crazy situations, considering my past track record. Enough is enough. Well, Jason was no different than the others.

At first Jason appeared to be normal, whatever that is. But before I knew it, the freak side slithered out. And there I was, once again in the midst of a dilemma. I was totally unsuspecting, so trusting, and then I looked over at this person that I was dining with, and could have sworn I could see tiny horns growing out of his forehead.

It always starts off slowly, the dos and the don'ts. The suppers we had agreed upon for the exchange of lower rent, twice a week, was changed to three to four. The vacuuming, dusting and the bathrooms were upgraded to twice a week, instead of once. All demanded without a discussion, just given as an order, like you are an indentured slave and not a roommate.

Looking back, I believe it was his intention to date me. Hoping that once I moved in I would like him more. Maybe even fall in love with him.

After I had been living there for about a month, he actually accused me of trying to come into his bedroom at night!

"The door was opened. Where you trying to get into bed with me?" he said.

"I would never do that," I said to him calmly. Thinking to myself, NEVER, EVER, YOU CREEPY, CRAWLY HOT MESS!

"You must have gotten up at night and forgotten to close the door," I said in a motherly tone. It was like trying to comfort a child who had had a nightmare. This was certainly not in the agreement!

It seemed like I had gone from one unhealthy living situation to another. My lack of money lent itself to desperation. When you are making these decisions, you don't look carefully or clearly and read between the lines, you are in survival mode, as I was. Here we go again.

TWO WHOLE MONTHS after I moved in, May actually, Jason announced to me about his very new religious convictions. He was in fact becoming a Mormon. A MORMON! I have nothing against the Mormons really, just Jason. You cannot make this stuff up.

Evidently, he had been contemplating this religion for a few months and now he was sure that this was what he truly wanted to become. He also told me that the ELDERS stated that I could not live in the same house with Jason unless we were married.

LOVELY, just lovely!

"What?" I yelled back, the shock and disbelief choking me. "I just moved in March and now you are saying I have to LEAVE?" My voice rose with every word. "Isn't this something you could have discussed with me before I moved in? I have no place to go. Nowhere! What am I supposed to do? This is so unfair! So unfair," I went on, my anger ignited by the pure madness of this new twist.

I felt like smashing something, throwing something. And if it accidently careened into him, OH WELL!

"I'm so very sorry Kathy. I know I should have told you about all this, but I wasn't sure at the time if I wanted to become a Mormon. Now I know that I do. I really do, and I hope that you can understand."

"I don't understand at all. I am baffled. To leave this Mormon thing out was so careless, and mean too!

"I want to speak to these ELDERS. Next time they come here I want you to arrange for me to meet with them, I have to talk to them and let them know how their decision will affect my life."

WITHIN A FEW days Jason had arranged for a meeting with the Elders. ELDERS my ass, these were young men, no older than late twenties! Well, at least they had agreed to the meeting.

I tried to calm my emotions, to look at the situation from their standpoint. Deep breathing, counting to ten and a prayer were the weapons I would use in this discussion, battle if you will. I didn't want to appear hostile.

The doorbell rang at the scheduled time for the Elders to arrive. Jason went to the door to let them in. The usual pleasantries were exchanged, you know, "Good evening. Come on in. We can all sit down in the kitchen to talk."

Jason then escorted them into the kitchen. I followed cautiously, trying very hard to maintain a friendly composure. We shook hands and exchanged the usual generic greeting, and sat down at the table, Jason choosing to excuse himself from the meeting.

"Coward," I said to myself, as he left me all alone with the two young Elders. He almost *ran* out of the room.

I began, "Thank you for hearing me out on this important matter. I understand you have a problem, or rather your religion, with men and women sharing housing unless they are married."

"Yes, that is our belief," the taller of the two Elders responded.

"You also believe that men and women cannot be friends," I continued, "and just be roommates."

"That is also true," the shorter of the elders chimed in. "We believe that you would tempt Jason into having sex with him."

I could feel my blood start to rise already. I took in a few deep breaths to calm myself down a bit. I didn't want to be too calm though, I needed some of the boil to say what needed to be said!

"Listen," I raised up my voice a few notches, wanting to get the Elder's full attention, "If Jason is tempted by ME living in this house, then it is JASON'S problem, not mine! He offered me a place to live, a place to call home. I just left a crazy situation, and now I found myself in another? I have no place to go if you kick me out! I just wanted you to know that."

In a condescending tone, the taller Elder responded, "We completely understand your view of this, however we do not agree. So, if Jason chooses to become a Mormon, then you must leave."

It was then that I realized that this was not a discussion, this was a lecture. It was pretty much their way, or no way. It didn't really matter what happened to me.

In one last attempt to let them see my side of the story, I retorted, "Would Jesus have kicked me out of my home?"

There was silence for a few moments. They did not have anything to say to what I had just said to them. They just looked up from staring at the floor, and finally said, "We're sorry."

They showed themselves to the door. Jason still hidden away in his bedroom on the second floor. I was the one with the balls now.

MEN!

A WEEK OR so after, the Elders called Jason telling him that some Mormon woman had found a place for me to live. It was a Mormon lady that had a room for rent not far from Jason's condo. I could just call the Elders and they would arrange for me to meet her.

Funny what a guilty conscience can do. Throwing crumbs to the poor women who is HOMELESS now because of YOU. I don't think so! I want the main course of life, nothing less!

"No thank you," was my answer to the crumb.

Once again reasons, seasons, lifetimes. "Every experience is a success," says author Louise L. Hay in her book, *You Can Heal Your Life.* I guess there was something I needed to learn about the Mormon faith, and I did. I never wanted to become one!

At the end of April my daughter Kristen and I had decided we would move in together. Kristen was living in Worcester, MA at the time and was going to go back to school to finish her Graphic Design degree.

We were both in a tough spot, and this would be a way to cut down on the expense of living alone. I had met Kristen's landlord in March of 2006. He told me that he had lots of income properties, and to call him when we were ready to move. So, we did. We were both SO ready!

MR. D SHOWED us a lovely little abode on 169 Wayne St. Well, lovely to us anyway, because it was a haven compared to where we both were living. I take that back, it's not where you live, it's who you live with.

The stairway as we ascended to the available apartment on the second floor was extremely shabby. However, once he opened the door, our eyebrows raised. It was better than we expected.

The cozy dwelling had three small bedrooms. The smallest one was in between, which was perfect for an art/office room. The living room, kitchen and pantry were all perfectly lined with hardwood floors. There was a good-sized bathroom with a tub and a shower, and a toilet of course. And off the kitchen, to the north, there was a porch.

As Mr. D. finished up the tour, we looked at each other and smiled. We almost started to jump up and down for our seemingly good fortune. We refrained, however; too much excitement could lead to a higher rent for us.

"I like it. Just big enough for the two of us," I said.

"It's in good shape, and the pantry is just off the kitchen, it will be a great place to cook," Kristen stated in a calm manner.

"So, how much can you afford right now for the rent?" Mr. D. asked us.

We were both silent for a moment, not believing our ears. He was asking US how much WE could afford. What?

Honesty was the best policy. First, we asked what would be included in the rent.

"It includes just heat," Mr. D replied. We didn't respond. I know I was thinking about what my financial status was, and I knew I couldn't afford any more than $350.00 per month, without the utilities. I looked at Kristen, and I could see that she was also calculating her ability to pay as well.

"We need to take a second look," I told Mr. D.

So Kristen and I did a second tour on our own as Mr. D waited in the kitchen area for our return. We were definitely interested, but didn't want to show our joy on the outside. Kristen was already whispering to me that the bedroom facing the south was the one she was claiming. And in the living room area she was planning where the leather couch she had could go.

I liked the bedroom on the north side of the apartment, just off the kitchen, with one window facing the west. I looked out that window, curious to see the view, only to see the back alleyway and another apartment building about 40 feet away. Close, but acceptable.

We headed back to the room that Kristen was calling her bedroom. We looked at each other and smiled from ear to ear, did a silent shaking dance, gave each other a high five, then slowly walked back to where Mr. D. was.

Down playing our excitement Kristen said nonchalantly, "I guess this will do. We'll take it for $700.00 a month."

"Okay. It's a deal," Mr. D. replied. He then presented a lease from out of the manila envelope he had been carrying. We used a pen with blue ink to sign the form to seal the deal.

"Here are two sets of keys. This one is for the front entrance, and this one is for the back." He then handed a set to Kristen, and then one set to me. It was one of those frozen moments in time. We had our own place! Finally! We deserved a break that would make it okay for all the shit we had been through. Mr. D. left a few minutes after that.

Kristen and I lingered a little after he left. Letting the reality of this set in for a bit. Looking around, checking out each room a little more in depth. We embraced each other as happy tears filled my eyes.

"This is our new home. I'll start moving my things in. Wow." I jumped up and down like a child getting the gift she wanted for Christmas. And, even though it was May, it felt like December. Home is not a place it is a space, where your spirit surrounds itself with joy and enthusiasm. And although fear tries to kill it, with faith, it will never die.

It was another adventure for us, living together, neither one of us making a clear decision. One made out of desperation and lots of faith. And the beat went on, still more to learn.

With a broken smile, and my invisible, magical, ruby red slippers, I moved along. Tapping my heels together three times I said, "There is no place like home."

Believe Nothing,
No matter where you read it
Or who had said it,
Not even if I have said it,
Unless it agrees with your own reason
And your own common sense.

Buddah

PART THREE:

THE AFTERMATH

TWENTY-EIGHT

IT WAS INEVITABLE that something was going to give. You don't thrive with elegance when the skeletons in your closet have endured abuse, neglect, abandonment, physical abuse, alcoholism and rape. Life doesn't become easy because you are free from jail. Being a felon brings is a difficulty that few people understand who have not lived it.

As I related earlier, ywo weeks before my court date I was fired by the company that had employed me for almost a year. Why? There were no work issues. However, once the owner found out my offence, courtesy of a local popular newspaper, my employment was swiftly terminated. Evidently, I was considered a liability now because I would have a record.

The unknown, the fear, dug its talons deep into me. I would know what my fate would be soon. Unfortunately, now, I could add unemployed to my resume.

Why was employment such a worry?

After I left the courtroom on July 24, 2002 the judge delivered my sentence. I would be on probation for three and a half years and have to attend court ordered counseling for one year. It would cost me about $40.00 per month for being on probation. The counseling would be $100.00 a month, for a total of $140.00, to be paid in full every month, or be incarcerated.

If I hadn't suffered enough from guilt fear and shame, my cup runneth over now. The guilt of what I had done to my daughters and myself. Fear of rejection, of joblessness, of homelessness, and retaliation from the predator, and the fear of being overcome by PTSD once again.

The shame of it all was suffocating most of the time. For several years after the June 14th incident I stayed away from places where I might run into anyone that might know me. A neighbor, a co-worker or acquaintance could trigger me and send me to the floor in a fetal position.

Once I was in a grocery store and ran into an old neighbor. She froze when she saw me, as I did in turn. The look on her face said it all. It screamed "FELON, run and hide from this crazy lady. She shot a gun at a man." Never mind that she had known me for years before it happened.

Anyway, she managed to force out a shaky "Hello." Then she slowly asked me "Are you okay?" Not really wanting an answer, but desperately wanting to run away. I answered, "Doing well." Then she responded with, "That's good." She grabbed her cart and mumbled, "I've got to go," and sped off. This was someone that I had been well acquainted with from working on the PTA where our children attended school.

To be feared like that cut right through to my soul, and tears filled up my eyes. Her reaction crushed me. The realization that all the good that I had done in my life didn't matter to some people, but the one isolated incident did. I wanted to lay down on the floor and die. I was devastated.

At the next job that I acquired, I was a dedicated employee. I worked six days a week there so that I could afford a studio apartment. All of a sudden on the Monday after Mother's Day I was fired. I had in fact trained the NEW GIRL myself, not knowing that she was my replacement. There was no notice given. I was disposable because he had gotten all he needed from me.

That door closed, but another better one opened up. I could not surrender my dignity to the system I had fallen prey to. So, I called an old boss who knew me. Who really KNEW me, knew all the details surrounding the first degree assault. Well, without any hesitation, he hired me back! My eyes filled with tears as I lay in bed that night. They were tears of validation. I did have value, and he remembered!

A few years later that place went out of business. Once again, I was in that terrible, horrible hole of unemployment. A wave of panic and fear washed over me, actually a debilitating fear. The lack of money when you are living week to week affects where you live, what you eat and where you can go.

Also, while on probation I had the fear of being put back in jail if I didn't pay the monthly probation fee and the counseling fees. I could barely afford the basic essentials, never mind the court ordered expenses.

For the next ten years, I felt overwhelmed most days. My situation was so oppressive. I felt like I was branded like a slave, and I still do sometimes. I had created more fear, more shame and guilt for myself, and I felt like I was suffocating. I just wanted to go to sleep forever, so I attempted to kill myself at least three times.

For years I had to endure asshole bosses who belittled me, especially those employers who knew that I had a felony. They took advantage of the situation because they could. They could smell my desperation to keep my job, the perpetual fear of being homeless looming over you. So you crawl to almost every request, even though you know that you are disrespecting yourself.

You remain silent to your roommate's tantrums and rules. You are a roommate, after all, because you cannot afford your own place. You don't want to be kicked out, because you don't have anywhere to go but to the street.

As a felon, I have become more of a doormat, more complacent and numb. You don't use your voice because you are petrified of the repercussions.

I didn't drink. I wasn't on any street drugs or prescribed medications so the blunt force trauma of it all wasn't stopped. Thank goodness I read the works of great authors like Wayne Dyer, Oprah Winfrey, and Louise Hay to empower me with their words of wisdom. It wasn't one day at a time sometimes, it was one second at a time!

My coping mechanisms: running, yoga, eating well and sleeping to calming meditative music at bedtime, were all extraordinary components of deep healing. I had to be brave and strong to thrive. I never gave up. I started to believe that God was on my side. Instead of focusing on my issues, I started to focus on the possibilities of life.

I was finally able to considerably overcome my fear, guilt and shame. Time definitely helped me to heal my scars, to embrace my past and TOSS IT. My faith and my daughters brought me to a great place, a place where I found good work, good housing, where I can live and not just exist. I made it home.

Home is being able to live in the moment. It is living with acceptance, enjoyment and enthusiasm every single day. It's learning to "Not mind what happens," because that creates resistance. Where life is life, it's not good or bad, there are no labels. You free your mind and your soul. You are just being, and that is HOME. And, there is no place like home!

The tsunami came and went, and like any tsunami, it left in its aftermath lots of pain and suffering. So it was up to me to pick myself up time after time. To rise above it all and know that I was worthy of having the best life!

Winston Churchill, who I admire greatly, led the British people in their darkest hours. He never gave up. One of his famous quotes was, "Success is stumbling from failure to failure with no loss of enthusiasm."

After all these years I still have my enthusiasm. I know in my heart who I truly am, and I own it! That is all that really matters, to live in love, and not in fear.

I understand the grave importance of physical and mental health. I have triggers of people and situations that I have eliminated from my life. Unfortunately, you can't always eliminate mean miserable people, who are hurting and want to hurt you.

A few months ago, I was catapulted back to my past offense. Recently, I became a grandmother for the very first time. It was pure delight for sure. I was happily discussing with a friend my new role and how I couldn't wait to babysit when the new parents went out.

Well, without skipping a beat she said, "Are they going to let you babysit? You know, because of what you did?"

In the Name of Love

It's been over 19 years since my offence, none before, none after and those words actually spewed out of her mouth like acid, her harsh words passing judgment on me again. If she was my friend, she would have never said that to me. If she didn't know me by now, she never would! Words meant to hurt and crush my joy. In that instant I was transported back to that moment in time, and all the pain it included.

I took a few deep breathes. I realized that this verbal attack was not about me, it was about her pain. Once again cruelty and meanness are the problems of that person. And within a few days I was able to easily remove the fear, guilt and shame layers, I tossed them, then I moved on.

Now after years and years of struggling I finally found good work with good pay. Work that I am proud of. I have a nice place to live where I feel safe and happy most of the time. "Progress, not perfection."

I take time to sit and look around my apartment. Happy tears of joy fill my eyes. I made it! I did! And I have a box of tissues in every room to dry them.

ACKNOWLEGEMENTS

Merci, Go raibh maith agat, Grazie, no matter how you say it, in any language, when you say "Thank You," you are expressing gratitude. And, even though I am the author of *In the name of Love*, there have been many who have stood behind me, holding me up, supporting my hands to write, to type. So many people, with their unconditional love, helped to bring my book to fruition.

First of all, I am so grateful for my oldest daughter, Kristen. Her creativity, adventurous spirit, and love have set me free on the path to be me again. Layers of guilt, fear and shame have melted away because of her strength, courage and ability to say yes to life, without any regrets. A special thanks also to my daughter, Sarah. She has always brought her wit and charm into my sometimes floundering life. She has taught me to laugh at the world. Especially at the darkest of times, laughter always lightens you burdens, and brings the light back into your world again.

When I think of gratefulness, I say a great big THANK YOU to Karen Lesko, a dear friend who has stood by me through all the joys and sorrows. Relentless, by my side, to listen, to encourage and to inspire me, and who still talks to me even though she knows the good and not so good about me.

To Judy Puchaz and Leslie Peterson, whom I have known since third grade, and although we don't see each other often, I can call them up, and we pick up where we left off. Amazingly, their love and support has been there for me, Kathleen Rioux, through tears and laughter.

A big round of applause and a supersized THANK YOU goes to Michael Mckinnon. Countless adventures, planet fitness workouts, hiking and biking, have provided me with the necessary therapy I so desperately need to carry on sometimes. And when I don't, we just have fun. Like the lighthouse in the harbor, he has guided me back home many times through the storms of life.

A special thanks to Ed Hudson for supporting me with his

expertise on computers and their programs. He assisted me in putting my old mare of a computer out to pasture, only to replace it with a stallion, a laptop. His kindness, encouragement, and patience, was of tremendous help in getting to the finish line with this book.

Lastly, I would like to extend a huge heartfelt THANK YOU to Tom Holbrook. He has been a constant positive force for me. His professionalism, patience and perseverance in helping this book come to life is greatly appreciated. He fine-tuned my story, so it became music, not noise!

It has been quite a ride, indeed. But I am grateful for every single experience of my life. I try to be present, and to live in the moment. I am living, and will never give up, and I will let love be my tour guide for the rest of this journey.

www.ingramcontent.com/pod-product-compliance
Lightning Source LLC
Chambersburg PA
CBHW022122080426
42734CB00006B/222